WELCOME TO CYBERSCHOOL

Culture and Politics Series
General Editor: Henry A. Giroux, Pennsylvania State University

Postmodernity's Histories: The Past as Legacy and Project (2000) by Arif Dirlik
Collateral Damage: Corporatizing Public Schools—A Threat to Democracy (2000) by Kenneth J. Saltman
Public Spaces, Private Lives: Beyond the Culture of Cynicism (2001) by Henry A. Giroux
Beyond the Corporate University (2001) edited by Henry A. Giroux and Kostas Myrsiades
From Art to Politics: The Romantic Liberalism of Octavio Paz (2001) by Yvon Grenier
Antifeminism and Family Terrorism: A Critical Feminist Perspective (2001) by Rhonda Hammer
Welcome to Cyberschool: Education at the Crossroads in the Information Age (2001) by David Trend

Forthcoming:

Surpassing the Spectacle: Global Transformations and the Changing Cultural Politics of Art by Carol Becker
Dangerous Memories: Educational Leadership at a Crossroads by Barry Kanpol
The Politics of Ethics by Jacques Derrida, edited and introduced by Peter Pericles Trifonas
Growing Up Postmodern edited by Ronald Strickland

WELCOME TO CYBERSCHOOL
Education at the Crossroads in the Information Age

David Trend

ROWMAN & LITTLEFIELD PUBLISHERS, INC.
Lanham · Boulder · New York · Oxford

ROWMAN & LITTLEFIELD PUBLISHERS, INC.

Published in the United States of America
by Rowman & Littlefield Publishers, Inc.
4720 Boston Way, Lanham, Maryland 20706
www.rowmanlittlefield.com

12 Hid's Copse Road, Cumnor Hill, Oxford OX2 9JJ, England

British Library Cataloguing in Publication Information Available

Library of Congress Cataloging-in-Publication Data

Trend, David.
    Welcome to cyberschool : education at the crossroads in the Information Age / David
Trend.
        p.   cm. — (Culture and politics)
    Includes bibliographical references and index.
    ISBN 0-7425-1563-X (alk. paper) — ISBN 0-7425-1564-8 (pbk. : alk. paper)
    1. Computer-assisted instruction.   2. Internet in education.   I. Title: Welcome to
cyberschool.   II. Title.   III. Series.
    LB1028.5 .T63   2001
    371.33′4—dc21
                                                                            2001019529

Printed in the United States of America

♾ ™ The paper used in this publication meets the minimum requirements of American
National Standard for Information Sciences—Permanence of Paper for Printed Library
Materials, ANSI/NISO Z39.48-1992.

Contents

1. Politics, Technology, and School   1

2. Utopian Promise and the Digital Divide   17

3. The Education Business   45

4. Welcome to Cyberschool   65

5. Myths of Cyberdemocracy   85

6. Reading Cyberculture   115

7. Broken Promises and Democratic Possibilities   143

Index   155

About the Author   159

1

Politics, Technology, and School

IN THE UNITED STATES, education has a special place in the national imagination. Years ago, schooling was viewed as a critical tool of democracy, functioning as both a social equalizer and an enabler of civic agency. In a land purporting to afford opportunity to every citizen, access to schooling was regarded as an important vehicle for social mobility. Indeed, for many new immigrants and working-class people in the nineteenth and early twentieth centuries, education was idealized as the route to the American Dream.

In more recent decades, education has enjoyed a less exalted image, as the great social equalizer has been cast as the source of social, economic, and even moral decay in the United States. Beginning with the famous Reagan-era report *A Nation at Risk*, schools have come to be characterized as bloated public bureaucracies populated by incompetent teachers who allow standardized test score averages to drop below those of our international competitors. Although less than informative about the actual causes of the nation's educational ills, *A Nation at Risk* remains remarkably instructive about the ways conservative bureaucrats conceive of knowledge as human capital. In this scheme, aggregate test scores are indicators of national wealth and grade-point averages the credentials for career entry. Competition and individual achievement are stressed over community values and the common good.[1]

In the years following *A Nation at Risk*, conservatives have ridiculed liberals in dozens of similar policy documents for throwing money at the problem of educational failure, as both camps looked toward more privatized and cost-efficient administrative models. School districts began engaging local business people for management advice, and corporate CEOs assumed university presidencies. Education may not have improved during this period, but its failings certainly were no longer due to fiscal excess. In the "tough love" climate of 1980s school funding, federal school policies lost whatever liberal bent they had, as funding from Washington was systematically reduced. With less federal money, local school districts were obliged to depend more on local property tax revenues—which vary wildly from region to region. This exacerbated the differences between impoverished and wealthy schools, as inner cities, rural regions, and other economically disadvantaged areas fell further behind well-off communities and the suburbs. Typically this meant that the gap widened between White and non-White schools, and between those that were technology-rich and those that were technology-poor. Naming this condition one of "savage inequalities," Jonathan Kozol said that progressive redistributive efforts had been "turned back a hundred years."[2]

Soon more profound changes occurred. As offspring of the baby-boom generation began to enter the classroom in the 1990s, debates over education shifted from assignments of blame to prescriptions for improvement. With government deficits turning into occasional surpluses, a renewed sense of urgency returned to educational policy discussions. Suddenly everyone had ideas about how to fix schools by testing teachers, firing administrators, tinkering with admissions, offering vouchers, or promoting school choice. Joining the cacophony of voices were religious leaders, politicians, radio talk-show hosts, academics—in short, just about everyone except parents and students. If the debates yielded anything, they demonstrated how multidimensional a problem effective educational reform turned out to be.

Further complicating these discussions was an overriding belief that "technology" could help somehow. With the meteoric growth of high-tech companies and their contribution to the nation's economic recovery, technology became the solution to every problem. Despite subsequent instability in the "dot-com" marketplace, this faith in technology persisted. Of course, the idea of mechanized instruction was hardly new. In the 1920s and 1930s, audiovisual materials such as sound recordings, slides, and films were used widely in K–12 schooling with the support of the National Educational Association. The new field of educational psychology supported the use of these new media because they were believed to improve students' experience of school and enhance their ability to memorize concepts.[3] Significantly, these early proponents of technologically mediated education saw themselves as progressive reformers, not unlike the current promoters of computerized learning.

Schools of the Future

In 1996 President Clinton declared his intention to wire every classroom to the Internet and to make computer literacy a part of every child's education.

Joining the high-tech cheering section were administrators touting computers as a means of increasing teacher productivity and stimulating student learning. Outside the classroom a media frenzy was taking place, with new reports of the booming "information economy" amplified by an explosion in advertising for computer companies, software developers, Internet providers, and technology investment opportunities. All of this instilled in many parents a fear that without computer education their children would be left behind educationally and compromised economically. In the K–12 arena, this triggered a reassessment of matters ranging from school funding to curriculum design. Similar changes began occurring at the college level as well.

As technology reentered the classroom, it opened the door even further for the business community. This was partly the effect of the bottom-line orientation of educational reform, which encouraged schools to adopt a more competitive, market-driven approach. Yet more significantly, the corporate world began to recognize the potential of education as a market. The educational investment firm EdVentures estimates the market in schools at between $630 billion and $680 billion.[4] Of course, education had always been good business for textbook publishers and school furniture manufacturers. With the 1990s emphasis on computerized instruction, it became feasible for corporations to move from the margins of educational merchandizing to the center of course design, curriculum planning, and school policy. Corporations were quick to capitalize on this new access to education. Within a decade, schools became much more than sites of product placement and sales for the technology industry, as districts across the nation began developing industry-friendly classes, providing free labor (in the form of interns) for business, and training ready-to-hire employees.

The beginnings of this phenomenon made news several years ago when Christopher Whittle's infamous Channel One made its debut in K–12 education. In exchange for a range of audiovisual and computer equipment provided by Channel One, schools would require students to watch a daily twelve-minute "news" segment peppered with ads for Pepsi and Nike. Channel One is now seen by 40 percent of young people in secondary schools in the United States. Following this example, cash-hungry local school districts now permit promotional materials on school buses, corridors, and textbooks—and Taco Bell and Wendy's have taken over cafeteria franchises. "Underfunded schools, desperate for resources, are increasingly receptive to corporate-sponsored educational materials and programs, and are ever more accepting of the associated commercialism and product promotion," observed Peggy Charren of the advocacy group Action for Children's Television.[5] Recent examples are truly disturbing. In Jefferson County, Colorado, Pepsi gained the exclusive right to market its products in 140 schools by donating $2 million to build a high school stadium. Elsewhere third graders are learning math by counting Tootsie Rolls as older students are studying business by viewing materials about how a McDonald's restaurant is run.[6]

Once the sacred preserve of local communities, schools and school policy are often developed and "operationalized" by profitmaking corporations, but financed by municipal and state governments. The most common approach is through the charter-school process adopted by many states in recent years, which makes it possible for any entity—parent group, community organization, or profitmaking corporation—that presents a credible plan to open a school underwritten in large part by municipal funds. In this new environment of "public/private partnerships," school has become a product for which one shops. Sometimes it is a bargain, sometimes not.

The Digital University

The union of education and business is most profoundly evident in higher education, where course delivery, curricular content, academic research, and even the structure of educational institutions are driven by a plethora of corporate agendas. What was born in the 1980s as the telecourse model of delivery, largely used by community colleges, mushroomed in the 1990s into a profusion of Internet-based entities like the University of Phoenix. With more than fifty thousand students in seventy cities, the University of Phoenix is now the largest private university in the nation. The Virtual University of California and fifteen-state consortium of the Western Governors University have constructed similar online degree-granting services, as have a growing number of less reputable entities.[7] In almost all cases these new computerized campuses share a number of characteristics: a shift of instruction to off-site satellite branches or to an online "virtual" campus, a mechanization of noninstructional services, and a move away from career faculty.

What is driving the university's headlong rush to implement new technology with so little regard for the pedagogical and economic costs, and at the risk of student and faculty alienation? In "Digital Diploma Mills: The Automation of Higher Education," David Noble comments,

> A short answer might be the fear of getting left behind, the incessant pressures of "progress." But there is more to it. For universities are not simply undergoing technological transformation. Beneath that change, and camouflaged by it, lies another: The commercialization of higher education. For here as elsewhere technology is but a vehicle and a disarming disguise.

To many observers, universities have fallen victim to a predatory capitalism, with administrators the willing accomplices of the digital corporation. But a simple materialist critique of the situation doesn't explain entirely what's happening. Often corporations gain ground in universities for seemingly reasonable purposes. For one thing, colleges are feeling intense pressure from high-tech corporations seeking computer-competent employees. This is especially true of two-year institutions. As the high-tech world begins to drive colleges in a more vocational direction, a growing number of proprietary institutions (once called trade schools) are competing with traditional institutions for students. At first glance, the reasoning seems solid. We inhabit a postindustrial "information society" in which intangible goods like images and ideas are the prime commodities—and people who can produce them represent the workforce of the future. These sentiments received official endorsement in 1992, when then-U.S. Labor Secretary Robert Reich wrote in his *The Work of Nations: Preparing Ourselves for 21st Century Capitalism* of the coming need for what he termed *symbolic analysts*.[8] These were individuals Reich described as "continually engaged in managing ideas" and who "solve, identify, and broker problems by manipulating symbols."[9] A decade later stories abound in mainstream press about the booming high-technology industry, its creation of instant millionaires, and its hunger for appropriately trained employees. The U.S. Commerce Department recently issued a report titled "America's New Deficit: The Shortage of Information Technology Workers," which opens by asserting that "the sweep of digital technologies and the transformation to a knowledge-based economy have created a robust demand for workers highly skilled in the use of information technology. In the last ten years alone, employment in the U.S. computer and software industries has almost tripled."[10] Using data from the Bureau of Labor Statistics, the report argues that the number of jobs in main information technology categories (computer programmers, scientists, and analysts) will grow from 1.3 million in 1994 to 2.1 million in 2005.[11] These highly technical job categories are not affected by fluctuations in Internet commerce or stock prices, such as those that occurred in early 2001.

But what about the rest of the workforce? While the information technology sector swells, what about the nation's other 125 million nonfarm employees? In other words, what about the other 98 percent of workers? Although the Bureau of Labor Statistics confirms that technology *as a category* is growing more quickly than others, this category represents a relatively small cohort of the overall workforce.[12] Larger, less glamorous, categories of employment are where the bulk of new jobs actually exist. In the coming years the bureau projects that most new jobs will be those of cashiers, health care workers, salespeople, and truck drivers. Already, 21 million people work in manufacturing, 18 million in retail, and 7 million in transportation.[13] This means that although the rapidly growing but minuscule digital employment sector contributes to the perception of economic prosperity, the most dramatic growth in new jobs remains in low-wage, low-skill categories.

During his presidency, Bill Clinton warned workers that they would need to retrain themselves six or seven times during their careers to keep up with rapidly changing technology in the workplace. But how reasonable is this admonition? How fair is it to oblige 125 million citizens to reinvent themselves every five years to satisfy the high-tech job market? While corporations are profiting from their ability to close factories and manipulate the global workforce, the majority of the nation's families are working longer hours for lower wages and generally struggling to make ends meet. Although by some definitions, operating a cash register at McDonalds constitutes "working with a computer," it is hardly the sort of employment that generates a living wage.

Just as the frenzy over technology jobs changed the university's teaching mission, it profoundly affected other functions as well. Like the shift toward vocational training, some of these transformations had been years in the making. The character of academic research changed in the 1970s, when universities began to feel budget cuts caused by the nation's then-faltering economy. Like other nations of the industrialized world, leaders in the United States recognized that the nation could not maintain its monopoly on heavy industrial production. Unionized domestic labor was just too expensive. Future monopolies needed to evolve from "knowledge-based" industries producing what was termed *intellectual capital*.[14] Companies turned to universities to supply this new commodity, and the cash-strapped educational institutions quickly gravitated to the new arrangement.

With the 1980s came unprecedented political pressure to privatize all aspects of education. This created an atmosphere for more extensive relationships with the business community, and it set the stage for the quantum expansion of corporate sponsorship resulting from the computer revolution. Market demands for ever newer, more powerful, and complex technology tools made product research extremely lucrative. In many instances this led to dramatic expansions of university research initiatives. But it also produced a downside, as academic institutions gradually decreased support for projects that lacked a potential financial payoff. This is especially true for disciplines in the arts and humanities. But it also affected the social sciences and other "soft" disciplines.

In some ways this infusion of money and technology has changed the very structure of academic institutions. For example, networked instruction allows institutions to serve dramatically more students while investing minimal resources in a physical plant. Operating largely from rented office space, the University of Phoenix has no tenured faculty and no faculty unions with which to contend. The Western Governors University will outsource much of its instruction to "nontraditional educational providers, such as corporations that train employees for specific skills."[15] WGU is developing relationships with profitmaking third parties to provide library materials and counseling services to students who "may be located anywhere," with corporate partners including Apple, ATT, Cisco Systems, IBM, Microsoft, Novell, and Sun, among others.[16]

As computers become recognized as machines that service every aspect of university life, old divisions within the university become softened. On the positive side, computers can facilitate relationships among previously disconnected areas, thus breaking down the often artificial boundaries that separate academic disciplines. This implies not only new syntheses of knowledge, but new efficiencies in the sharing of resources. Regrettably, administrators frequently recognize this latter benefit, only to transform it into the driving force behind cross-campus collaborations. As Noble puts it,

> Major promoters of this transformation are university administrators, who see it as a way of giving their institutions a fashionable forward-looking image. More importantly, they view computer-based instruction as a means of reducing their direct labor and plant maintenance costs—fewer teachers and classrooms—while at the same time undermining the autonomy and independence of faculty.[17]

In a similar sense, the interdisciplinary character of computer technology is inspiring new initiatives, programs, and departments or the transformation of existing efforts into entities that serve the agenda of the information-age university. This raises obvious questions in educational institutions with static budgets. What is lost, devalued, or defunded as new programs are put in place? Whose agendas are served? How can the growth and restructuring resulting from information technology be used to change the character of an institution? To rework its values?

To many observers, the incursion of digital media into the college classroom and research laboratory signals nothing less than an assault on the humanistic principles that brought many people to the university. What of the education of the whole person? Not only can teaching via machines promote alienation among student "customers," it also frequently fosters forms of one-directional instruction that stifles (or at least discourages) student participation or inquiry. On a more personal level, mechanized instruction guts education of many of its underacknowledged values. As Michael Bérubé has observed,

When you're "teaching" 10,000 students by satellite or over the Internet, there's no way you can grade their papers, counsel them on their courses, work with them on their prospective careers, or write them letters of recommendation for jobs and postgraduate programs. Personal, individual contact with students is one of the most costly and inefficient services a university can provide. It is also one of the most valuable—and the most educational.[18]

Knowledge and Power

Serious as this assault may seem on the educational mission of the university, it might well represent a much broader challenge to humanistic social values. After all, schools and universities do much more than convey facts and methodologies. Educational institutions at all levels serve as pedagogical systems through which students are socialized to recognize and internalize ways of acting in other situations. Clear parallels exist between the structured environment of the classroom (with schedules, tests, and grades) and that of the workplace (with time clocks, evaluations, and pay). These underlying attitudes toward authority were what educational theorists of the 1960s and 1970s termed the *hidden curriculum* of school. Naturally the influence of the hidden curriculum is rarely absolute, as evidenced in the ways people mentally accept, contest, or reject the information they receive. Nevertheless, systems of education go a long way in shaping what people count as meaningful, what they internalize in the form of values, and what they respect in terms of authority.

None of this is a secret. The fundamental role of school in the shaping of society has been the subject of political debates over education and much of the related "culture wars." But oddly, technology has remained immune from such considerations—considered by most people on both sides of the political aisle to be an unquestionable necessity. Kevin Robbins and Frank Webster take a different view, arguing that behind the media hype about technology in education lie other motivations. To Robbins and Webster, what is pushing computers into the classroom is a new desire for social control that will make people more easily manipulated by corporations. As workers, companies want individuals who are more flexible about when they work and what they do—employees who monitor and retrain themselves, but disappear without expense when not needed. This desire reflects the flexible or "post-Fordist" (post–assembly line) operation of technology-based multinationals, favoring temporary, part-time employees, who are called when needs arise, and who must continually adapt to changing production needs. According to Robbins and Webster, schools have responded with instructional programs that look like this:

- the teaching of competencies and skills rather than traditional subjects;
- experiential, project-based and problem-solving pedagogy rather than didactic academic methods;
- individualized learning contracts in which students assume responsibility for their own development;
- increased orientation to the work of business and industry;
- emphasis on technological and computer "literacy";
- a focus on personal and social as well as technical and vocational education;
- a commitment to "life-long learning," defined as a routine of re-education and re-training throughout one's working life.[19]

Viewed in terms of educational politics, this would appear to be a very progressive program, rooted in student-centered learning, collaboration, schooling in everyday life, and learning outside the institution. All of these were things conservative reformers of the 1980s hated. But Robbins and Webster argue that the hybrid "progressive instrumentalism" represented by this model is hardly so benign, especially when workers are linked via office/home computer networks. Rather, this new set of arrangements constitutes a contemporary manifestation of the "panopticon" prison discussed by Michel Foucault.[20] In the panopticon, prisoners become so accustomed to being watched that they come to watch themselves. "What might appear to be innovative and progressive developments toward self-regulation are, we maintain, fundamental to the panoptic model,"[21] Robbins and Webster write. " 'At once surveillance and observation, security and knowledge, individualization and totalization, isolation and transparency,' (Foucault) remains the paradigm for social control."[22]

The Digital Divide

Such analyses of power rarely find their way into policy debates these days. Instead, proponents of cyberschool argue that the powerful wave of digital technology that created so many millionaires in Silicon Valley has the ability to transform life as we know it. Tempered briefly by the tech stock meltdown in 2000 and 2001, the techno-class of *digerati* (digital literati) or *netizens* (citizens of the Internet) clings to its faith in a resurrected "new economy" and shows little patience for any skepticism about its vision of utopia. Amid an increasingly contradictory groundswell of ads and news accounts, the ability of cyberspace to generate insight, connectedness, and security is privileged over the way cyberculture might erode equality, community, and social justice. This thinking is reproduced in dozens of similar magazines, Web sites, and advertisements in mass circulation publications. In *Data Trash: The Theory of the Virtual Class,* Arthur Kroker and Michael Weinstein write about the newly emergent class of digital enthusiasts "typified by an obsession to the point of hysteria with emergent technologies, and with a consistent and deliberate attempt to shut down, silence, and exclude any perspectives critical of technotopia."[23]

Appropriating a 1960s language of "freedom" and "equality" in touting the benefits of cyberspace, the digerati rhapsodize over the pending saturation of Internet coverage that will soon connect everyone on the planet. During the last decade, the number of Internet users worldwide has risen to approximately 350 million, the majority of whom reside in the United States and other Western industrialized nations. This means that Internet users represent less than 6 percent of the world's six billion people. Even if projections are correct that Internet use will double in the next few years, the fact remains that it is a far from ubiquitous medium. Simply put, while a minority of the world's population is moving into a virtual society, with all of the attendant benefits, the rest of humanity remains in a world of material scarcity. As increasing amounts of commercial and cultural activity are shifting to the Internet, the distance between the connected and the unconnected may well be creating a new global information proletariat. That unconnected world knows little about modems, satellites, computer laptops, or the Internet. Although it is rarely, if ever, discussed in the discourse of digital culture, more than half the people in the world do not even have telephone service.

Indeed, on many levels the vast expansion of information technology has created what the U.S. Commerce Department has termed a *digital divide.* The Commerce Department reports that low-income households were twenty times less likely to have Internet access than those of the middle and upper classes. People with little education were 25 percent less likely to be netizens than those with high levels of education. Rural residents were half as likely as urban dwellers to count themselves among the digerati.

The academic and scholarly community has been relatively silent on these issues. While occasionally acknowledging that the Internet replicates existing relations of commerce, popular spokespeople for the electronic frontier, such as Mitch Kapor, John Perry Barlow, and Benjamin Wolley, generally overlook the imperialistic, logocentric implications of this new space, as well as the way the "real" world continues to define who people are and what they can do. As such, the silence contributes to the consolidation of commercial and residential capital in the nation's Silicon Valleys, while producing growing transient or ghettoized populations in urban areas or in the nations of the developing world that produce most of the world's silicon chips.

Accompanying the high-tech consolidation of economic capital is a comparable consolidation of cultural capital. The worldview of most people already is profoundly shaped by the information they receive in electronic formats. As digital media become the prime conduits for personal communications, business transactions, and entertainment of all kinds, the commodification of cyberculture becomes synonymous with the commodification of human experience. Soon the Internet will merge the function of telephone and television, merging "private" and "public" forms of communication in a single device. With this phenomenon, formerly separate realms of human communication will be joined in a medium controlled by the profitmaking impulses of corporations. As Jeremy Rifkin explains,

> After thousands of years of existing in a semi-independent realm, occasionally touched by the market but never absorbed by it, culture—shared human experience—is now being drawn into the economic realm, thanks to the hold the new communications technologies are beginning to enjoy over day-to-day life.[24]

The transparent way that technology has entered our lives has permitted the obfuscation of politics or the refusal to acknowledge them. Although lip service is sometimes paid to electoral politics via the "electronic town meeting," the tendency of both popular and academic writers is to focus on cyberspace in an extremely romantic sense. Whether the goal is adventure or community, the overriding ethos evokes a traditional Platonic metaphysics in which ideal forms are privileged over material objects. For some writers this focus on the "poetry" of cyberspace is its essential rationale. Digital technology becomes the means of achieving the transcendent and unified subjectivity that has been the desire of Western philosophy for centuries.

Often this translates into an inexplicable mysticism, a belief in the ability of the digital to locate hitherto unreachable territories of knowledge and consciousness. Brenda Laurel, artist and author of the book *Computers as Theatre*, states that digital expression serves "to conjure up transformative powers, to propel us beyond the boundaries of our minds and push our cultural evolution into new territories."[25] Similarly, cyber-guru Jaron Lanier states that cyberspace "gives us a sense of being able to be who we are without limitation," permitting "our imagination to become objective and shared with other people."[26] By emphasizing the idealized character of digital environments, these writers deny the way space in the "real" world continues to define who people are and what they can do.

Cyberdemocracy

Democracy has emerged as another theme in the romanticization of cyber-technology. Like education, digital media and new forms of communication are regarded by many as means of leveling social inequities and erasing problematic differences. Much as Marshall McLuhan predicted a "global village" wired like the human nervous system, in which instantaneous communications would obviate misunderstanding and conflict, proponents of the Internet and its related technologies suggest that cyberspace will exercise a magical cure for a plethora of social ills.[27] As Al Gore has put it, "Our new ways of communicating will entertain as well as inform. More importantly, they will educate, promote democracy, and save lives. And in the process they will also create a lot of new jobs. In fact, they're already doing it."[28]

Such rhetoric constitutes yet another way in which cyberspace is credited with utopian powers to generate insight, connectedness, and prosperity, while allowing us to forget or deny the forces that mitigate against equality, community, and social justice. Overlooked in this discourse are the many ways that technology is used by government, corporations, and individuals for purposes ranging from surveillance to profiteering. In this context, the promotion of virtual education and cyberdemocracy can be viewed as little more than another way in which technology becomes abstracted from the human relations surrounding it and idealized as an autonomous force.

Central to the discourse of cyberdemocracy is a view of the Internet as a community—as a virtual place where people meet, chat, conduct business, or develop a sense of togetherness. These relationships are developed on demand, at the touch of a switch, from the distance of a remote screen. An unabashed advocate of the social potentials of these "virtual" encounters, Howard Rheingold says, "People in virtual communities do just about everything people do in real life, but we leave our bodies behind."[29] For obvious reasons, the idea of virtual communities is attractive in certain political circles. This was the fundamental premise behind Ross Perot's vision of national "electronic town meetings"—an idea later advocated by such political opposites as Newt Gingrich and Dick Morris. This notion of a giant national conversation holds enormous popular appeal, for it satisfies both the affective desire for an inclusive community and the "commonsense" notion that such a unified common culture is possible and advisable. It goes without saying that the virtual crowd also leaves behind such bodily inconveniences as hunger, poverty, and violence in the pursuit of electronic comradeship.

The "virtual" character of online communities has generated a growing skepticism about their true utopian prospects. Some critics argue that these simulated communities really aren't communities at all, but more resemble games or performances. As Ziauddin Sardar comments,

> Real community creates context. It generates issues which arise with relations to time and space, history and contemporary circumstances, and requires responsible judgment—which is why so many issues are difficult, they require balancing of opposing pressures. A cyberspace community is self-selecting, exactly what a real community is not; it is contingent and transient, depending on the shared interests of those with the attention span of a 30-second sound bite.[30]

Harsher critics of virtual communities say they actually damage people's sense of community by diverting attention from social problems in the material world. The overarching question in this regard is whether it is possible for a technology to create new structures or understandings of life, without first altering the fundamental power relations and social organizations in which the technology operates. Is the Internet capable of changing the way people conceive their relations to one another? If so, is it ever possible for such new understandings to escape the historical and cultural baggage from which they emerge? Or is it more likely that the most new technologies offer are more varied ways of addressing the world as it exists?

Given the identification of Internet providers and computer manufacturers as multinational corporations fully participating in the inequitable distribution of information technology worldwide, it seems unlikely that cyberspace will bring about the democratization of the globe anytime soon. Once again, the essentially expansionist character of the capitalistic enterprise cannot be overstated. It is the single most powerful force in contemporary technological society and it is ruthless in its drive. In recent decades the marketplace has assumed the place of government in many areas of public life. Profitmaking companies commonly operate public utilities and mass transportation systems; malls and fast food "play areas" are replacing parks and neighborhood recreational facilities. If virtual communities exist in any sense, it is as multinational corporations that use computer networks to manipulate labor markets, facilitate plant closures, enable just-in-time production, capitalize on currency fluctuations, subvert import/export regulations, and generally exploit less powerful populations around the world.

The critical issue in this simulation of community is the way it pretends that it is something different, thus encouraging people to invest their trust in these new Internet communities. The most significant difference that cyberspace communities embody is their orientation as commercial entities through which access is advertised, metered, and delivered at a price. Although this once might have been an insult to the average citizen, the commercialization of everyday life has become accepted and expected in an age in which most social speech reaches citizens through advertising rather than any other means. For this reason, the critique of cyberspace cannot be limited to the realm of technology. Digital culture demands scrutiny as a social, economic, and political construction. More to the point, the effects of new technology need to be measured on scales of human ethics and values. Is it possible to reconcile the democratic aspirations of cyberspace with its inegalitarian materiality? Perhaps. But not until digital media become widely regarded as a terrain of struggle rather than inherently innovative, educationally progressive, or democratic spaces. Otherwise, the utopian rhetoric of cyberspace will continue to generate little more than false hopes and broken promises.

Notes

1. National Commission for Excellence in Education, *A Nation at Risk: The Imperative for Educational Reform* (Washington, D.C.: U.S. Government Printing Office, 1983).

2. Jonathan Kozol, *Savage Inequalities: Children in America's Schools* (New York: Harper-Perennial, 1991), 4.

3. See Anne De Vaney, "Can and Need Educational Technology Become a Postmodern Enterprise?" *Theory and Practice* 37, no. 1 (Winter 1998), 72–80.

4. Julie Light, "The Education Industry: The Corporate Takeover of Public Schools," *Corporate Watch*, www.corpwatch.org (6 November 1999).

5. Peggy Charren, quoted in Holley Knaus, "The Education Industry: The Corporate Takeover of Public Schools," *Corporate Watch*. www.corpwatch.org (6 November 1999).

6. Steven Manning, "Students for Sale: How Corporations Are Buying Their Way into America's Schools," *The Nation* 269, no. 9 (27 September 1999), 11.

7. Lisa Guernsey, "Is the Internet Becoming a Bonanza for Diploma Mills?" *Chronicle of Higher Education* (19 December 1997).

8. Robert Reich, *The Work of Nations: Preparing Ourselves for 21st Century Capitalism* (New York: Vintage, 1992).

9. Reich, *The Work of Nations,* 85, 178.

10. U.S. Department of Commerce, *America's New Deficit: The Shortage of Information Technology Workers* (Washington, D.C.: U.S. Commerce Department, 1999), 1.

11. U.S. Department of Commerce, *America's New Deficit.*

12. Bureau of Labor Statistics, *National Industry-Occupation Employment Matrix* (Washington, D.C.: U.S. Department of Labor, 1999).

13. Bureau of Labor Statistics, *National Industry-Occupation Employment Matrix.*

14. Bureau of Labor Statistics, *National Industry-Occupation Employment Matrix.*

15. Michael Margolis, "Brave New Universities," *First Monday* 3, no. 5 (4 May 1998), n.p.

16. Margolis, "Brave New Universities."

17. Margolis, "Brave New Universities."

18. Michael Bérubé, "Why Inefficiency Is Good for Universities," *Chronicle of Higher Education* XLIV, no. 13 (21 November 1997), B4.

19. Kevin Robbins and Frank Webster, *Times of Technoculture: From Information Society to the Virtual Life* (London and New York: Routledge, 1999), 173.

20. Michel Foucault, *Discipline and Punish: The Birth of the Prison* (Harmondsworth, UK: Penguin, 1979), 249.

21. Robbins and Webster, *Times of Technoculture,* 179.

22. Robbins and Webster, *Times of Technoculture,* 179.

23. Arthur Kroker and Michael A. Weinstein, *Data Trash: The Theory of the Virtual Class* (New York: St Martin's Press, 1994).

24. Jeremy Rifkin, *The Age of Access: The New Culture of Hypercapitalism, Where All of Life Is a Paid-For Experience* (New York: Putnam, 2000), 138. See also: Michael Margolis and David Resnick, *Politics as Usual: The Cyberspace "Revolution"* (Thousand Oaks, Calif.: Sage, 2000); Ann Travers, *Writing the Public in Cyberspace: Redefining Inclusion on the Net* (London and New York: Garland Publishing, 2000).

25. Brenda Laurel, *Computers as Theatre* (Reading, Mass.: Addison Wesley Longman, 1993), 385.

26. David Tomas, "Old Rituals for New Space: Rites and Passages in William Gibson's Cultural Model of Cyberspace," in *Cyberspace: First Steps,* ed. Michael Benedikt (Cambridge, Mass.: MIT Press, 1991), 32.

27. Marshall McLuhan, *Understanding Media: Extensions of Man* (New York: New American Library, 1964).

28. Al Gore, as cited in Peter Kollack and Marc A. Smith, *Communities in Cyberspace* (New York and London: Routledge, 1999), 4. See also: Stephanie Gibson and Ollie Oviedo, eds., *The Emerging Cyberculture: Literacy, Paradigm, and Paradox* (Cresskill, N.J.: Hampton Press, 2000); Beth E. Kolko, Lisa Nakamura, and Gilbert R. Rodman, eds., *Race in Cyberspace* (London and New York: Routledge, 2000).

29. Howard Rheingold, *The Virtual Community: Homesteading on the Electronic Frontier* (Reading, Mass.: Addison Wesley, 1993), 3.

30. Ziauddin Sardar, as cited in Andrew Calcutt, *White Noise: An A-Z of the Contradictions of Cyberculture* (New York: St Martin's Press, 1999), 22.

2

Utopian Promise and the Digital Divide

CYBERCULTURE PROMOTES a utopia made possible by technology. Pick up any newspaper or magazine, or turn on a television, and you will see endless advertisements and news items suggesting that the latest digital phone, palm computer, minidisk player, or chip-implanted credit card will yield increased productivity, enlivened leisure time, and enhanced communication—not to mention social harmony, economic stability, and democracy.[1] Unlike prior utopias brought about by philosophical reflection, social amelioration, or proletarian revolt, this version of the future is a product of a different sort. With the purchase of the appropriate products and services, a perfected existence will come from a multinational corporation.

This vision isn't so new, really. Throughout history, business interests have cloaked their agendas in a rhetoric of social betterment. General Electric's familiar "better living through technology" mantra of the 1950s was really just another way of focusing consumer attention on the added convenience of electric frying pans, blenders, and dishwashers—and away from the specters of industrial pollution, nuclear annihilation, and the forces of predatory market capitalism. Indeed the purpose of advertising has always been to sell the idealized images that lie behind commodities, rather than merely the products themselves. In our hypersaturated media environment, the relationship of representations to their referents becomes reversed. Commercial images do not represent products, as much as products represent images.[2]

So what, if anything, is new about the utopia offered by cyberculture? In part, the answer lies in the extent to which this utopia is endlessly hyped and promoted. But in another sense, digital media present novel and not entirely understood modes of experience that extend subjectivity, social relations, and political power into increasingly ephemeral and elusive dimensions. As people spend more and more time with their telephones, televisions, and computers, the physicality of experience diminishes. This has specific consequences for the world of commerce, where the production and sale of goods and services increasingly moves from the material to the immaterial. Concepts and images—termed *intellectual capital*—now dominate a marketplace previously devoted to the exchange of objects. The old economy, in which goods were bought and sold, is giving way to a new economy, in which commodities are accessed and networked. Meanwhile, computers and digital networks have created enormous new markets for Internet providers, software developers, and e-commerce entrepreneurs—to name but a few. Although the pace of this transformation was broken somewhat by the tech stock deflation in late 2000 and early 2001, the growing ubiquity of computers and the Internet is undeniable. In this environment, new currencies emerge relating to speed, access, and privacy. How fast a connection can one afford? How much hardware is needed? Where, when, and at what price can one access information? At how many points are one's movements and choices observed, recorded, analyzed, and sold?

In this hyperbolic atmosphere, power and politics become more difficult to see. In the view of David Rodowick, this invisibility produces an environment in which forces of social control have become vaporous or liquid. Struggles over space and material are now waged over ideas and time. No longer the structural monoliths of modernist thought nor the scattered capillaries of postmodernism, power in digital culture is ubiquitous and dynamic, flowing in currents around us. This encourages a certain collusion, as agents find themselves floating or surfing among various currents rather than stopping the tide or stepping outside of it. As Rodowick puts it, "Agency means that one no longer invents, but rather capitalizes on the existing current. The most one can do is anticipate and navigate the flows and directions."[3] There are two dangers here. On one hand, in an atmosphere where one feels powerless to do anything more than navigate among currents, simply giving up, giving in, or dropping out begins to seem like a reasonable option. This is the sentiment of the alienated voter, the cynical consumer, or the isolated suburbanite. On the other hand, when politics and social relations migrate to a world of pixels and bytes, a tendency develops to discount their importance as mere "cultural" phenomena.

These latter ideas dogged the cultural studies movements of the 1990s, as critiqued by writers like Pam Rosenthal, who argued that "culture promises, at best, to give narrative and symbolic coherence to popular questions and anxieties. It does not promise structural solutions; historical and political analyses and practice—history, in a word, is what's supposed to do that."[4] Without discounting the basis of such arguments, it is important to acknowledge the very genuine possibilities for individual and collective agency that digital culture offers. Without drifting uncritically into the nostalgic yearning for the "virtual community" of Howard Rheingold and his followers, it is important nevertheless to acknowledge the communitarian ethos that makes such thinking so popular today. Although the communities enabled by online conversation, list-serves, multiple-user dimensions (MUDs), Web rings, and virtual environments should not be mistaken as equivalents of experience and political life in the material world, their power to reflect and constitute that world should not be discounted.

Speeding with Paul and Bill

A recent advertisement appearing in *Wired* magazine depicts an anxious-looking twenty-something man, dripping wet, peeking from behind a shower curtain, with the caption "A lot has happened while you were off-line." The ad then describes the range of information-gathering tools available through the new "DeveloperWorks" service. Such practices typify the way high-tech corporations encourage the nervous excitement about rapid technological change that characterizes cyberdiscourse, in this instance suggesting that even five minutes away from a workstation might result in a devastating loss. The wry suggestion that one should never stray from one's digital tether is captured with irony in a similar Macintosh ad that reads, "Now you can access your office from wherever you happen to be. Bummer."

Paul Virilio has written that "speed" has become a driving metaphor in the accelerating world of cyberspace, especially as conveyed through advertisements. Like the computer itself, speed can have positive or negative consequences. For Virilio, speed produces a setting in which "systems of telecommunication do not merely confine extension, but that, in the transmission of messages and images, they also eradicate duration or delay."[5] The result is a "fundamental loss of orientation" in time and space, a point of both possibility and vulnerability.[6] The disorientation allows one the sensation of breaking free from conventional physical and metaphysical constraints, while producing a destabilization that opens one to confusion, manipulation, and error.

But corporations rarely leave anything to chance. Although the DeveloperWorks ad may prey on the anxieties produced by the "fundamental loss of orientation," the real strength of the message lies in the certainty with which it posits rapid change. This ethos of acceleration is nowhere more bluntly articulated than by Bill Gates in his best-seller, *Business@the Speed of Thought*. Gates writes,

> If the 1980s were about quality and the 1990s were about re-engineering, then the 2000s will be about velocity. About how information access will alter the

lifestyle of consumers and the expectations of business. Quality improvements and business-process improvements will occur far faster. When the increase in velocity is great enough, the very nature of business changes. To function in this digital age we have developed a new digital infrastructure. It's like the human nervous system.[7]

It's easy to understand why Gates believes this. Capital growth and product development in the information technology industry continue to move at unprecedented rates, with the network economy doubling every nine months.[8] Many in the industry speak of the technology advancing in "dog years," meaning that seven years are compressed into one. Sun Microsystems' Eric Schmidt similarly uses the expression *web weeks* to describe the pace of research, adding that most Internet-related innovations become obsolete within a year.[9] But not only business is changing, according to Gates. Along with a range of technocrats, pop philosophers, politicians, and plain old hucksters, Gates proclaims the total transformation of society and human consciousness. "Your workplace and your idea of what it means to be educated will be transformed, perhaps almost beyond recognition." He adds, "Your identity, of who you are and where you belong, may open up considerably. In short, just about everything will be done differently."[10]

Sound familiar? To a great extent Gates is simply repackaging the aphorisms of his corporate ancestors in promoting the revolutionary potentials of the latest appliance or gizmo. This kind of thinking took a quantum leap in the 1960s, however. During that era, Canadian professor Marshall McLuhan developed a cultlike following in his futuristic prognostications about the potential of numerous existing and emerging technologies—from the lightbulb to the television. But perhaps his most celebrated thinking involved what would later become the Internet. McLuhan envisioned what he termed a "global village" in which the world would overcome antagonism via the agency of perfect communication.[11]

> Electric speeds create centers everywhere. Margins cease to exist on this planet. . . . Our specialist and fragmented civilization of center-margin structure is suddenly experiencing an instantaneous reassembling of all its mechanized bits into an organic whole. This is the new world of the global village.[12]

This message had a powerful, affective appeal in its suggestion of world peace and egalitarianism at a time of nuclear proliferation and political protest. In today's atmosphere of the "New World Order" the technological means of accomplishing McLuhan's vision has actually materialized—but without its 1960s idealism.

Not surprisingly, Gates links almost every change and presumed improvement to the computer, specifically the networked computer. This is what brought him unprecedented success and wealth, after all. A critical element in his program is the presumption of a type of transferability of his good fortune—the idea that via technology and an understanding of *Business@the Speed of Thought,* anyone can share in the dream. Indeed much of the book is a how-to manual for using the Internet to increase business efficiency, monitor employees, and respond to customers. But when stripped of its high-tech window dressing, the volume is simply another instance of crediting technology for a range of very nontechnological ideas. Gates asserts that with an in-house intranet, "the worker is no longer a cog in the machine but is an intelligent part of the overall process."[13] But certainly no computer network can create such relationships where the will is missing. In a similar vein, responding quickly to complaints delivered on postcards or e-mail amounts to the same idea. Yet Gates persists in the suggestion that technology offers a radical utopia.

> We are all created equal in the virtual world, and we can use this equality to help address some of the sociological problems that society has yet to solve in the physical world. The network will not eliminate barriers of prejudice or inequality, but it will be a powerful force in that direction.[14]

At the time of this writing the personal net worth of Bill Gates was estimated at $72 billion, making him the richest man on the planet. In comparative terms, this means that Gates's wealth is equal to that of the entire lower half of the U.S. population—or 140 million people. Extrapolating on the rate of return Gates has experienced on his money thus far, *Wired* magazine recently estimated that Gates would become the world's first trillionaire in 2005.[15] In crude monetary terms, equality in the virtual world does not mean equality in the material world.[16] But it would not be in the interest of Microsoft or IBM to admit that this is the case. Instead, Gates in his friendly and helpful persona as a writer (as opposed to his vicious and destructive persona as a monopoly capitalist) stresses only the most positively instrumental implications of technology. To Gates and his friends, the logic of their success is incontrovertible, larger than individuals, groups, or even nations. It is certainly more powerful than anything so quaintly nostalgic as the democratic process.

Founded in 1975, Microsoft grew to a company netting $279 million by 1990. Then something unprecedented occurred. Due to the skyrocketing growth of the Internet and PC sales, Microsoft profits grew to nearly ten times their 1990 level in just six years, to $2.2 billion. By 1999 profits had reached $7.8 billion with overall revenues of almost $20 billion. The recent growth is due in large part to the success of Microsoft in suppressing or buying out competition, a phenomenon that has resulted in a string of monopoly and unfair-business practices lawsuits by the Justice Department and numerous state attorneys general, not to mention individuals, corporations, and "classes" of complainants. In addition to an army of lawyers to defend its interests, Microsoft has gone on the offensive with a public relations effort in the form of an entity called the Freedom to Innovate Network (FIN). Calling itself a "non-partisan, grassroots network of citizens and businesses," FIN appears dedicated to recasting the mechanics of predatory capitalism in a language of individual rights and, of course, progress.[17]

As serious as the Microsoft monopoly is for the domestic economy, the more sobering story lies abroad. The most significant growth area for Microsoft—now accounting for 53 percent of all profits—lies in the overseas market. Not that the going has been all that easy. As in the United States, governments overseas are embroiled in numerous legal battles to restrict the growing hold that Microsoft has on computer and software sales worldwide. In Gates's rhetoric, such efforts are but misguided attempts to slow the pace of progress. Unacknowledged is the zero-sum reality that for every economic winner, there must also be a loser. In an age of multinational capital this means that the widening gap produced by information technology between rich and poor people has also become manifest in a growing divide between rich and poor nations. In 1960 the income of the people in the world's wealthiest 20 percent of nations was 30 times that of the poorest 20 percent. That ratio grew to 60-to-1 in 1990 and widened even further to 74-to-1 in 1997.[18] Put in overall economic terms, in the 1990s the fifth of people living in the highest-income countries generated 86 percent of the world gross domestic product (GDP) as opposed to 1 percent among the fifth in the lowest-income nations. Which brings us back to Bill Gates, who paints quite a different picture of the world:

> The network will spread information and opportunity across borders to developing nations too. Cheap global communications can bring people anywhere into the mainstream of the world economy. Knowledge workers in industrialized countries will, in a sense, face new competition. . . . The net effect will be a wealthier world, which should be stabilizing. Developed nations and workers in those nations are likely to maintain a sizable economic lead, but the gap between the have and the have-not nations will diminish—great news for the countries that are behind economically. Starting out behind is sometimes an advantage. Some developing countries will never pass through the "industrialization" state with its attendant problems. They'll move directly to the information age.[19]

The Digital Divide

The business of information technology is growing exponentially. In the 1990s the Internet evolved from a specialized tool for academics to a popular medium for everyday use. In 1988 the Net was composed of less than 100,000 "hosts" (computers with direct access to the Internet). Ten years later the number of hosts had risen to thirty-six million, as the number of Internet users worldwide rose to 143 million. As dramatic as this sounds, it is important to recognize that Internet users represent less than 6 percent of the world's six billion people. Even if projections are correct that online users will number 700 million by 2002, the Internet will remain out of reach for the vast majority of the world's people.[20] Even as the digerati celebrate the growth of cyberspace, the fact remains that it is a far from ubiquitous medium. Indeed, on many levels the vast expansion of information technology has created what the U.S. Commerce Department has termed a *digital divide*.

In global terms, the digital divide begins with something as simple as phone access. In industrialized nations, the percentage of people with telephones—or what demographers term *teledensity*—is unusually high. For example, in the United States there are approximately 65 telephone lines per 100 people, compared with nations such as Afghanistan, Bangladesh, and Kenya, where there is less than one line per 100 people.[21] In South Africa, the African nation with the best phone service, 75 percent of schools have no phone lines, and at universities, up to 1,000 people share a single connection. It is estimated that such telephone-poor nations will take 50 years to match the line-density of countries like Germany or Singapore. Thailand has more cellular phones than the whole of Africa.

The United Nations Development Program (UNDP) states that the United States has more computers than the rest of the world combined. In fact, fifty-five countries account for 99 percent of global spending on information technology. With but 15 percent of the world's population, industrialized nations generate 88 percent of Internet use. North America, with less than 5 percent of the world's population, has 50 percent of all Internet users. By comparison, a region like South Asia, with 20 percent of the world's population, accounts for less than 1 percent of Internet users. This is more than a matter of access to a modern convenience. The Internet is quickly becoming the dominant communication medium for commerce and culture—and leaving large segments of the world's nations and people without access to this vital information source. Jeremy Rifkin says,

> When one segment of the human population is no longer able even to communicate with the other in time and space, the question of access takes on political

import of historic proportions. The great divide in the coming age is between those whose lives are increasingly taken up in cyberspace and those who will never have access to this powerful new realm of human existence. It is this basic schism that will determine much of the political struggle in the years ahead.[22]

Aside from geography and nationality, other factors influence Internet use. The UNDP says that in South Africa, Internet users have incomes seven times the national average. In Latin America 90 percent of those online come from upper-class income groups. A computer that would cost a United States resident one month's salary would require eight years of income from an average Bangladeshi. Education is another factor. Worldwide, one third of Internet users have at least one university degree, with much higher numbers in nations like China (60 percent), Mexico (67 percent), and Ireland (70 percent). Turning to gender, in the United States, the gap is still profound, especially among young people—with five times as many boys as girls using computers at home. Among adults in the United States, men account for 62 percent of computer users. The percentage of male users is even higher in nations like Brazil (75 percent), Japan (83 percent), South Africa (84 percent), Russia (93 percent), and China (96 percent). It's also worth noting that 82 percent of Internet culture is communicated in English, the language spoken by 6 percent of the world's population.

Despite egalitarian claims by entrepreneurs like Bill Gates, technology is enabling rich nations to get richer. Technology allows wealthy nations to conduct more research to more quickly develop more products to sell. Ten nations possess 84 percent of global research and development, own 95 percent of U.S. patents, and account for 90 percent of all cross-border royalties and licensing fees. Even content is unequally distributed. More than 90 percent of the data and statistical analysis about Africa are collected, stored, and disseminated in the United States and Europe. As a consequence, this information is largely unavailable to African researchers themselves. More to the point, what do the leading research nations produce?

In defining research agendas, money talks louder than need—consumer drugs and slow-ripening tomatoes come higher on the list than a vaccine against malaria or drought-resistant crops for marginal lands. Tighter control on innovation in the hands of multinational corporations ignores the needs of millions. For new drugs and better seeds for food crops, the best of the new technologies are designed and priced for those who can pay. For poor people, technological progress remains far out of reach.[23]

In general terms, the fifth of the world's highest-income nations produce 82 percent of goods purchased and control 68 percent of foreign investment, while the bottom fifth accounts for less than 1 percent in both categories. In 1998, just ten telecommunication companies controlled 86 percent of a $262-billion market. This latter statistic carries profound cultural implications in the flow of ideas and values from wealthy nations to poor ones. Few people realize that the biggest export of the United States is no longer weapons systems, computer software, or Coca-Cola—but entertainment. The U.S. television and motion picture business brings home more than $30 billion in revenues each year, an amount that promises to grow significantly through Internet broadcast.

The U.S. dominance of worldwide news and entertainment is more than an industrial phenomenon. It drives what Robert McChesney has termed the global *political economy of communication* as it has evolved in the twentieth century.[24] According to McChesney, before the existence of electronic media, politics and commerce operated on more local terms. Although the growth of "print capitalism" had done much to solidify the coherence of national borders and international trade, the near instantaneous communication made possible by radio and television enabled a new level of capacity for business and governments. Two other factors contributed to the modern political economy of communication: the increasing role of advertising as a supporting means of persuasion and the growing concentration of media ownership. Here McChesney credits the early writing on media consolidation by Ben J. Bagdikian in his often-quoted study of the 1980s, *The Media Monopoly*. Bagdikian described the near complete control of U.S. publishing by a handful of multinational conglomerates.[25] The book opens with the following ominous prediction:

> No single corporation controls all the mass media in the United States. But the daily newspapers, magazines, broadcasting systems, books, motion pictures, and most other mass media are rapidly moving in the direction of tight control by a handful of huge multinational corporations. If mergers, acquisitions, and takeovers continue at the present rate, one massive firm will be in virtual control of all major media by the 1990s.[26]

Although Bagdikian's dystopian vision has not yet been realized, there is striking evidence to support his claim. In print media alone, the statistics are staggering. In 1994, twenty major companies controlled more than half of the daily newspaper business. By the end of the 1990s, the number of companies was fourteen. Eleven companies controlled half of book publishing in 1994; by the end of the decade the number had shrunk to six. And the number of companies that control magazine publishing fell from twenty to three.[27] Due to overlapping interests among corporations involved in multiple areas, by 1996 twenty-three companies controlled virtually all print media. They include Capital Cities/ABC, Gannett, Harcourt Brace Jovanovich, Newhouse, *The New York Times,* Scripps–Howard, and AOL/Time Warner, among others. More significantly, the corporate directors of these media outlets also often sat on the boards of the very companies their magazines and newspapers would cover. As Bagdikian explains,

> This is more than an industrial statistic. It goes to the heart of American democracy. As the world becomes more volatile, as changes accelerate and create new problems that demand new solutions, there is an urgent need for broader and more diverse sources of public information. But the reverse is happening. Today there is hardly an American industry that does not own a major media outlet, or a major media outlet grown so large that it does not own a firm in a major industry. These media report the news of industries in which they either are owners or share directors and policies.[28]

When Bagdikian released his book in the early 1980s, fifty corporations controlled the nation's print, broadcast, and electronic media. In 2000, the number stood at six companies, led by the monumental AOL/Time Warner merger, which, with a value of $350 billion, was 1,000 times the largest merger of the 1980s.[29] The story doesn't stop there. Bagdikian's view of vertical integration has exceeded even his projection, as a company like Disney can produce a film for theatrical distribution, then distribute it on its own cable television stations and network, which will enable and promote musical soundtrack sales, which in turn will further support theme park rides and attractions, all of which will be refinanced and replicated in toys, books, games, and videocassette sales in outlets including, but not limited to, Disney's own chain of retail stores. Viewed from this perspective, the real value of a Disney film such as *The Lion King* (1994), which earned $600 million at the box office, lies in the vastly greater amounts that such supplementary markets and products yield—in this case more than $1 billion in profits.[30]

But more is at stake than money. According to McChesney, the ultimate result of the media monopolization of public communication is a mystification of politics and an erosion of democracy. The omnipresence of commercialism tends to undermine autonomous social organizations that can bring meaning to public life. "A capitalist society works most efficiently when the bulk of the population is demoralized and effectively depoliticized; when people have abandoned hope that social change for the better is even possible and therefore ignore public life, leaving the decisions to those at the top of the social pyramid."[31] In the international arena the American media monopoly exerts great influence over the culture and politics of other nations, especially those with underdeveloped media infrastructures. Beginning in the 1970s, people like Noam Chomsky and Herbert Schiller critiqued the way U.S. media exports functioned as components of a neocolonialist machine that kept nations of the developing world uninformed about foreign affairs, confused in their views of self-determination, and dependent on the United States for policy advice and guidance.

In the 2000s, this program of mystification replicates itself in claims that the Internet offers a "universal" medium in which differences in nationality, race, ethnicity, and language are subsumed within one global technoculture. Operating on the seventeenth-century premise of a universal grammar of pure mathematics, proponents of cybercommunitarianism from Howard Rheingold to Michael Heim posit a binary language of zeros and ones capable of perfect translation. The universal language would render all speakers equivalent (Rheingold) and all utterances intelligible (Heim).[32] Rheingold optimistically asserts that "as long as electronic networks are accessible to the entire population, easy to use, and legally protected as a forum for public speech, they have the potential to revitalize the public sphere."[33] Heim suggests that "we are more equal on the net because we can either ignore or create the body that appears in cyberspace."[34]

The most obvious flaw in this reasoning lies in the fact that the quite non-universal language of English, natively spoken by 6 percent of the world's population, is the language of 82 percent of Web communication.[35] This is hardly a new story. The idea of English as a universal language was asserted by the British Empire centuries ago to suppress indigenous languages and dialects in India and Africa, much as it continues to be deployed by the United States in the name of "New World Order." The point is that the blind assertion of *any language or medium* as universal denies the origin of that communicative form, the social structures from which it emerged, and any power dynamics attached to it. English is hardly a neutral or historically innocent language. Neither are photography and film. They all share the same ontological roots in Western systems of representation. Moreover, relegating utterances from diverse speakers to an ephemeral realm of universal language also denies the material circumstances (bodies, locations, and times) from which the communication comes. This practice stands as yet another way that the Internet offers a fantasy world quite different from the one in which real differences and inequalities exist.

As ubiquitous as the Internet has become, its role as a purveyor of "first world" market ideology is contradicted somewhat by its inherently distributed character—its lack of a center. On the other hand, when one considers the dominance of large corporations like Microsoft, CompuServe, AOL/Time Warner, and the growing wave of MP3-generation music and digital video providers—and the ease with which Internet communication crosses national borders—it becomes clear that the Net is already a hugely influential medium of popular culture. As the mergers and acquisitions continue that permit telephone, cable, and Internet services to consolidate into single corporations, the stage is being set for a dramatic narrowing of digital culture. Like telephone and cable, the Internet medium has been championed as a multivocal instrument for nonhierarchical and democratic exchange. And like those media, the Internet is rapidly being sectioned off and metered by the same corporate media monopoly that is already in place. Most Internet traffic already carries significant volumes of advertising. As such, the Internet is quickly becoming complicit in the perpetuation of global inequities generated by the broader news and entertainment industries.

Within the United States, the digital divide has become a topic of growing concern within government and academic circles. The U.S. Commerce Department's National Telecommunications and Information Administration (NTIA) first addressed the issue in a 1994 study compiled from census data. The initial research revealed significant disparities in computer and Internet use in relation to factors of education, race, economic class, and geographical location. Disturbingly, in a subsequent version of the study released in 1999, the NTIA found that while computer and Internet use had increased dramatically in general terms, some of the disparities had grown larger. Titled "Falling through the Net II: New Data on the Digital Divide," the report found that households with incomes of less than $25,000 were twenty times less likely to have Internet access than those with incomes of more than $75,000.[36] Nearly 17 percent of those without Internet access reported that it was too expensive. African American and Latino households were two thirds as likely to use the Internet as Whites. That gap has widened by 6 percentage points since 1994.

Several foundations have begun studying the digital divide. Research by the Markle Foundation found that significant portions of African American and Latino communities "reported not being aware of the internet."[37] Of those making that assertion, 58 percent reported household incomes of less than $25,000. A Benton Foundation report titled "Losing Ground Bit by Bit: Low Income Communities in the Information Age" underscores the role of telephone access in the digital divide.[38] Of the 6 percent of U.S. households that do not have phones, 43 percent receive public assistance and half are headed by women. African American and Latino families fall 10 percent behind White families in telephone access.[39] According to "Computers and Classrooms: The Status of Technology in U.S. Schools," a study conducted by the Educational Testing Service, students in poor committees had half of the access to computers in the classroom that their affluent counterparts had.[40] Schools with more than 90 percent of students of color had a student-to-computer ratio of 17-to-1, compared with the national average of 10-to-1.[41] To the Benton Foundation, these disparities in access and education add up to a disturbing conclusion:

> Even as digital technologies are bringing in an exciting new array of opportunities to many Americans, they actually are aggravating the poverty and isolation that plague some rural areas and inner cities. Advances in telecommunications are speeding the exodus of good jobs from urban areas to the suburbs, leaving inner cities and rural areas more isolated than ever from the kind of jobs, educational opportunities, quality health-care services, and technological services that they need to be able to contribute to the overall economy.[42]

Quoting California Telecommunications Policy Forum Chair Armando Valdez, the Benton Foundation warns that more may be at stake than the well-being of certain communities and groups. "We are witnessing the fracturing of the democratic institutions that hold us together," Valdez says. "The possibility of an information underclass is growing."[43]

Work in the Jobless Future

It is said that we now inhabit a postindustrial "information society" in which intangible goods like images and ideas are the prime commodities, and people who can produce them represent the workforce of the future. Currently 60 percent of all jobs require skills with information technology, a percentage that has been increasing at a steady rate in recent years. According to the U.S. Department of Commerce, 75 percent of all transactions between individuals and the government (such as food stamps and Social Security benefits) have been transferred to electronic methods.[44] This means that people who lack the ability to understand or use computers are severely compromised in both their employment likelihood and their ability to function without employment.

Surprisingly little has been written about these transformations of work and welfare, aside from enthusiastic proclamations in the popular media about job growth in high-technology sectors. One of the few scholars to address these issues is veteran labor historian Stanley Aronowitz, who has termed the current era a *postcritical period*—in reference to the frenetic technomania that so characterizes popular media. Aronowitz writes, "No doubt the main ideology of modern technologies is that virtually all of our problems—ethical, economic, political—are subject to technical solutions."[45] He attributes this problem to the difficulty of applying familiar ideological premises to computer-based media when both liberals and conservatives are gushing over the potential of new technology.

To Aronowitz, the most serious consequence of this political disorientation is a misunderstanding of the effect of new technology on work. As he frames the issue, "Celebrants of the new technological revolution engage in massive historical amnesia or, worse, have chosen to refrain from commentary on the major practical consequences of cybernetics: the destruction of labor."[46] This destruction takes several forms. On one hand the mechanization of certain tasks and the expansion of the "knowledge industry" have changed the character of labor. The replacement of factory workers with robots and bank tellers with ATM machines has meant that in certain sectors there are simply fewer jobs. The ubiquity of home computers and computer networks has transformed the space and time of work, with increasing numbers of home offices and the proliferation of part-time employment. Not so coincidentally, all of this has increased the profitability of corporations by allowing them to reduce workplace infrastructure, more tightly budget personnel time, and shrink the benefits and other supports that characterize full-time employment. The increasing atomization and distribution of the workforce also have made it less capable of organizing against management.

Because computers and their networks play such an important role in the linkage of work and home—in the erosion of the divide between public and private realms—it is not surprising that work is often a feature of computer advertisements. A recent Motorola ad features a photograph of a middle-aged and somewhat overweight car mechanic—something of an Archie Bunker type—in dirty coveralls and glaring unpleasantly at the viewer, with the caption "Who'd of thought that an electronic chip inside your car could help you avoid curbs, other cars, and best of all, Earl in repair." On one level, the ad is promoting the relatively recent innovation of global positioning systems (GPS) to help improve navigation and driving efficiency. But rather than illustrating the device directly, which would be somewhat difficult, the ad underscores the consequences of not having the device. Rather than showing the physical consequence of not having the Motorola chip, the ad confronts the viewer with an older, working-class White man. Certainly not a member of the digerati, the greasy palmed mechanic is portrayed as someone to avoid, scorn, or fear. And thanks to the chip, he is someone one will avoid. Indeed, Earl is exactly the sort of worker that digital technology has rendered redundant. In Motorola's future he will be gone.

Not that Earl is going to take this lying down. He represents a growing underclass of White male workers increasingly angered by a shrinking job market and about which they search for answers. Now forced to compete for a diminishing number of agricultural, manufacturing, and service jobs, this new White underclass blames affirmative action, immigration, taxation, and other government-related causes. As Jeremy Rifkin explains, "These men miss the real cause of their plight—technological innovations that devalue their labor."[47] Ironically, as the nation's income gap continues to widen and the character of labor deteriorates, the overriding message from the popular media and government is exactly the opposite. Stories abound in the mainstream press about the booming high-technology industry, its creation of instant millionaires, and its hunger for appropriately trained employees. The U.S. Commerce Department recently issued a report titled "America's New Deficit: The Shortage of Information Technology Workers," which opens by asserting,

> The sweep of digital technologies and the transformation to a knowledge-based economy have created a robust demand for workers highly skilled in the use of information technology. In the last ten years alone, employment in the U.S. computer and software industries has almost tripled. The demand for workers who can create, apply, and use information technology goes beyond these industries, cutting across manufacturing and services, transportation, health care, education and government.[48]

The report then states that there are 190,000 unfilled information technology jobs due to the "shortage of qualified workers" and that this number will grow by 95,000 per year through 2005. The document indicates that the number of jobs in main information technology categories will grow to 2.1 million by 2005. It says that although the number of students completing computer-related bachelor's degrees has risen significantly, there is a dramatic need for education to respond to this need. To alleviate this shortage, the federal government has launched myriad programs and incentives, including the mandate of the Goals 2000 Education Act that "U.S. students will be first in the world in math and science," the president's $2 billion Technology Challenge Grant program for schools, the Technology Innovation Grant Program for corporations and universities, and numerous school-to-work programs for community colleges and high schools. Clearly the federal government has heard the call of information technology companies for more workers.

Rarely is it acknowledged that the booming information technology sector accounts for less than 2 percent of the nation's workforce, much of which is poorly trained, overworked, and underpaid. While corporations are profiting from their ability to close factories, move operations, and take advantage of fluctuation in the global workforce, the majority of the nation's families are struggling to make ends meet. The Labor Department confirms that while technology as a category is growing, other less glamorous, yet huge, categories of employment are where the bulk of new jobs actually are situated. In the next five years, the largest overall growth in jobs will be in the area of cashiers, health-care workers, salespeople, and truck drivers.[49] The rapidly growing digital employment sector contributes to the more generalized perception of economic prosperity, when the most dramatic growth in terms of sheer numbers of jobs lies in low-wage, low-skill categories.

More to the point, those who find themselves outside the utopian digital workforce belong to the same social groups that have been traditionally left behind. Billing itself as a pure meritocracy in which skill is the only qualification for a job, Silicon Valley and other high-tech employment centers overlook the entrenched cultural biases that work against the advancement of certain social groups and the very pronounced gap that favors White workers—and to some extent male workers—over others. The *San Francisco Chronicle* reports that the Silicon Valley workforce is 4 percent African American and 7 percent Latino.[50] It is regrettable that this parallels national statistics. As indicated by David Bolt and Ray Crawford in *The Digital Divide*, "Only 5.4 percent of all computer programmers and 7.1 percent of computer systems analysts are African American. Latinos hold 4.6 and 2.5 percent of these jobs, respectively."[51] Writing of the Latino experience of high tech, Guillermo Gómez-Peña states,

> The myth goes something like this. Mexicans (and other Latinos) can't handle high technology. Caught between a preindustrial past and an imposed postmodernity, we continue to be manual beings—*homo fabers* par excellence, imaginative artisans (not technicians)—and our understanding of the work is strictly political, poetical, or metaphysical at best, but certainly not scientific. Furthermore we are perceived as sentimental and passionate, meaning irrational; and when we decide to step out of our realm and utilize high technology in our art (most of the time we are not even interested), we are meant to naively repeat what others have already done.[52]

These assumptions operate outside of the groups in question, but they derive from internalized racism as well. As John Ogbu explains, today's African American students often aren't drawn to science or technology because they don't expect to excel in such areas. In part, this derives from a belief that Whites (and to some extent Asians) hold a lock on these fields and that pursuing such knowledge means one is "acting White." Ogbu writes, "People think of math and sciences as something that white males do and for a black to succeed in these disciplines raises questions about his or her membership in their own group."[53]

Where does this thinking come from? One explanation is school, or rather, the profound inequities in the nation's K–12 school system. In high school, less than 6 percent of African American students take the kind of precalculus or science courses needed to prepare them for a technical major. Of those who do, fewer than 30 percent of those entering college in science or technology fields end up completing the degree (as opposed to 60 percent of Asian and White students).[54] These statistics result less from factors of attitude or expectation than from the opportunities provided for minority students. In California, more than 80 percent of African American, Latino, and Native American students find themselves in the poorest fifth of schools, where more than 25 students share each computer. Historically, these schools were last to receive computers and last to become wired to the Internet. These are schools where every dollar committed to technology represents a dollar subtracted from somewhere else, where choices have to be made between computer workstations and roof repairs. Clearly, differences in digital literacy and technological competence must be linked, at least in part, to broader issues of school inequality.

Content Gap

"There is no race. There is no gender. There is no age. There are no infirmities. There are only minds. Utopia? No, internet." This recent ad from MCI WorldCom typifies the corporate boosterism that posits the Net as colorless, carefree, and democratic. In the face of enormous disparities in Internet access and literacy, promoters of digital technology crassly assert its egalitarian character—even as they target their distribution to specific geographic locations and their advertising to specific market segments. It's no secret to residents of what have been termed Internet "dead zones" in states like Georgia, Mississippi, Maine, and Wyoming that low-density or rural regions are falling far behind the rest of the nation in their access to high-speed telephone lines. As the data contained in digital images, music, and video have increased exponentially, major metropolitan centers and high-tech enclaves have enjoyed access to lines capable of handling 56K or cable Internet services. According to statistics from Sprint, in New Jersey the average distance between a customer and the phone company's nearest switching facility is 2.6 miles, whereas in Wyoming it is twice as far and twice as costly.[55] Worse still, in isolated and rural areas it is often difficult or impossible to find an Internet service to provide local dial-up numbers. This adds long-distance charges to the already poor service available.

Just as access to computers and jobs has caused a digital divide in structural terms, the content of cyberspace creates a cultural divide. Not surprisingly, the two are mutually constitutive. A medium serving or connecting members of a specific group would be expected to convey the subjectivity of that group. Certainly in such arenas as e-mail, chat rooms, newsgroups, and other conversational forums, the participants overwhelmingly are young White men with disposable incomes. Most of the advertising on the Internet is selling either some form of technology (equipment, software, Internet services, or moneymaking tools) or recreation (travel, accommodations, games, gambling, or pornography). Whether online or in other related media, those pictured in Internet commerce are usually young White men or people addressing such an audience. A recent digital camera ad shows a twenty-something woman on a balcony blowing a kiss at the viewer. The caption reads, "You look up. She sees you. You don't look like a jerk fumbling with some other digital camera. Life is good."

These adolescent male sensibilities in advertising are supported by the broader cyberdiscourse that saturates society through movies, books, and games. Images of boys and men cruising around on spaceships or postapocalyptic motorcycles pervade the discourse in an endless stream of productions like *Star Wars, Bladerunner, Mad Max, Running Man, Max Headroom, Millennium, Terminator, Brazil,* and *Escape from L.A.,* to name but a few. Aside from a few notable interventions like *Alien* and *Deep Space Nine,* most films and television programs follow the same formulaic narratives as cyberpunk novels by William Gibson, Bruce Sterling, John Shirley, and Lewis Shiner. In this world of solitary and eternally embattled men, metaphors of the Old West abound, as in this description of the character Bobby from Gibson's *Burning Chrome*:

> Bobby was a cowboy. Bobby was a cracksman, a burglar, casing mankind's extended nervous system, rustling data and credit in the crowded matrix, monochrome nonspace where the only stars are dense concentrations of information, and high above it all burn corporate galaxies and the cold spiral arms of military systems. Bobby was another of those young–old faces you see in the Gentleman Loser, the chic bar for computer cowboys, rustlers, cybernetic second-story men. We were partners.[56]

On the surface, this evocation of the American Old West might be interpreted as an effort to humanize technology or render it in familiar terms. And familiar the narrative is—rendering the dystopian future in terms of a recognizable past, with all of its retrograde social roles and power structures in place. The real triumph of Gibson's writing has been the transformation of the image of the computer nerd or tech geek into that of the hip and sexy "hacker." Yet for all the radical pretensions of the hacker persona, its androcentric message of adolescent transgression offers little in the way of an alternative, aside from a boyish resistance. This is a primitive form of agency, to be sure, but one that is undirected and ultimately useful only as a diversion from actual politics or more complex human relationships. Jean Lave and Jane Wenger write, "It is no surprise that young males, with their cultural bent—indeed mission—to master technologies, are today's computer hackers and so populate the online communities and newsgroups."[57]

To many this masculinist discourse in science fiction entertainment is a simple extension of the gender bias in science itself. Sandra Harding and Donna Haraway, among other theorists, took issue with the claims of a technoscience grounded in assertions of purported objectivity. More often than not, scientific claims of universal truth did little more than mask the "unmarked" category of the male observer. In the ontology of Western science, women are constructed as an essentially distinct category, a premise originating from what has been termed the *one-sex model* in which the female body was understood as a lesser version of the male.[58] Such concepts provided a ground on which subsequent notions were based on women as weaker, more emotional, closer to nature, and fundamentally "different" from the male norm. This set women up as objects of male observation, study, and regulation through such "nonnatural" technologies as medicine, reproduction, and body modification. Barbara Katz Rothman writes,

> The Cartesian model of the body-as-machine operates to make the physician a technician, or mechanic. The body breaks down and needs repair; it can be repaired in the hospital as a car is in the shop; once fixed, a person can be returned to the community. The earliest models in medicine were largely mechanical; later models worked more with chemistry, and newer, more sophisticated medical writing describes computerlike programming, but the basic point remains the same. Problems in the body are technical problems requiring technological solutions, whether it is a mechanical repair, a chemical rebalancing, or a "debugging of the system."[59]

In his book *Science as Power*, Stanley Aronowitz describes the way scientific power develops from a conflation of knowledge and truth, a presumption that one kind of knowledge is the only source of truth. This stems from technoscientific claims of exclusivity in the possession of legitimate knowledge. Here technoscience behaves like religion in asserting that truth is self-evident and exclusively available through its internal architecture. In discursive terms, the process works something like this:

> First, the qualitative is excluded, or, more precisely, quality is occluded from the objective world; quantitative relations, expressed in the language of mathematics, have become the lingua franca of all discourse that claims knowledge as its content. Second is the imperative of empirical inquiry, which excludes

speculation except at the outset. Third, it is claimed that exact knowledge is free from value orientations, of interest. Fourth, method is given primacy in the confirmation of scientific knowledge.[60]

To Harding, this epistemology has implications far beyond those of gender alone. In addition to representing the narrow intellectual perspectives of a particular cohort of European men, this view enabled the exploitation of non-European nations in quite material terms. Global colonization depended on both the harvesting of natural resources from less-developed nations and their technological infantilization. This would result in countries that needed goods and services that they were incapable of producing. For example, Indian historians report the simultaneous introduction of European textile sales and the destruction of the Indian and Caribbean textile industries by British forces. Such practices produced an environment in which "development has been conceptualized in the North as the transfer of European models of industrialization—of European sciences and technologies—to the underdeveloped society of the Third World," Harding writes.[61] She adds ironically that contemporary postcolonial development studies "show that this kind of process has primarily de-developed the vast majority of people who were supposed to benefit from such science and technology transfers."[62]

The self-perpetuating and expansionist character of Western technoscience does more than simply generate convenient narratives that place some groups above others. In supporting and amplifying a fundamental self/other epistemology, it structures the way people come to understand who they are, how they can act, and what they can become. To return to cyberspace as a medium of communication, this self/other relationship is replicated in the way online communities are developing. In some instances this can be seen in quite specific patterns of behavior. Cameron Bailey has written of the way that online communications have developed a specific shorthand—or "netiquette"—with expressions like *BTW* (by the way) or *RTFM* (read the fucking manual). To Bailey these codes represent more than a more efficient way to communicate, for in them one can discern a means of forming a type of community that is specifically unfriendly to outsiders.

There is in these codes of language, and in the very concept of "netiquette," something of the culture of suburban America; one gets the sense that these structures are in place not simply to order cyberspace but to keep chaos (the urban sphere) out. It is not a stretch to suggest that in taming cyberspace, the white, middle-class men who first populated it sought refuge from the hostile forces in physical, urban space—crime, poor people, desperate neighborhoods, and the black and brown.[63]

Joseph Lockard similarly has remarked on the way that online communities seem to reinforce in discourse what they represent as structural entities, stating that "such internalized online monoculturalism reiterates the external racisms prevalent in American social structures."[64] He adds that "middle-class suburban America, confronted with its diversity on urban streets, has retreated to cyberspace to avoid the otherwise inescapable realities of diversity."[65]

What is even more interesting—or disturbing—is the way identity and difference of non-White people *are* represented. Within cyberliterature there is a frequently referenced cartoon in which a dog is seen at a computer. The caption reads, "On the internet nobody knows you're a dog!"— referring to the way the Internet allows one to hide one's identity or create fictional personas. This invisible rendering has caused Internet promoters like Bill Gates and others to champion cyberspace as a radically democratic medium that transcends race, class, and gender.

This phenomenon has complemented certain strands of contemporary theory, such as those developed by Judith Butler in her formulation of identity as performance. Numerous writers, predominantly feminists, have remarked on the liberating or subversive dimension of masquerading as imagined personas. Sherry Turkle has written extensively about one's ability to navigate in cyberspace through various encounters with other fictional characters. In her "Identity in the Age of the Internet" essay, Turkle writes, "Anonymously, I travel their rooms and public spaces (a bar, a lounge, a hot tub). I create several characters, some not of my biological gender, who are able to have social and sexual encounters with other characters."[66] Sometimes this takes an unusual turn. Turkle writes of her encounter in a multi-user dimension (MUD) with a Doctor Sherry, who possessed her background and research interests. This character, presumably constructed by one of Turkle's students, exemplifies but one of the numerous ways that identity performance can shift into identity theft, or something else. In either case, for Turkle this mutable character of identity on the Internet is something to be celebrated. But what does one's choice of a persona indicate? Like any other performance, Internet masquerade constitutes its own form of rendering or writing. It also conveys a degree of power, or at least the illusion of power in discourse. Sometimes this is exercised in a way that undermines the relative homogeneity of Internet users, as minority groups infiltrate the dominant discourse.

Nevertheless, when one "performs" an identity in cyberspace, what happens to the identity (or identities) one performs in offline situations? Does that latter self simply disappear? In their book *Race in Cyberspace*, editors Beth E. Kolko, Lisa Nakamura, and Gilbert R. Rodman argue that "real world" identity is connected to online identity in several ways.[67] They focus on race in asserting that a performance in cyberspace is simply that: a performance. It does nothing to change the author's ancestry, history of lived experience, worldview, or other factors through which an individual's racialized self is constructed. That racialized self informs the online persona and is always present. Unfortunately the connection between the persona on the screen and the persona animating that representation frequently is severed in discussions of online masquerade and in commercial references like MCI's "There is no race . . ." advertisement. This is the unfortunate legacy of purportedly "scientific" views of race originating in the nineteenth century, which focused exclusively on appearance. As Robyn Weigman has stated, "The visible has a long, contested, and highly contradictory role as the primary vehicle for making race 'real' in the United States."[68] Further complicating the view of a "raceless" cyberspace are the racialized depictions of characters in the growing body of movies about cyberspace like *Johnny Mnemonic, Hackers, Virtuosity*, and *Strange Days* in which all manner of familiar stereotypes migrate effortlessly into science fiction. Such media representations constitute yet another way that online identity is performed, as screen actors carry roles from cyberspace into the offline world.

It gets even more complicated. Nakamura has written of the way Internet users sometimes assume identities as oppressed or marginalized minorities in a type of twenty-first-century blackface. Terming this occurrence *identity tourism*, Nakamura reflects on the implications of crossing racial boundaries in such a temporary and recreational fashion. On one level this endeavor serves the purpose of tourism in general, which is to allow one to experience an exteriority—to be somewhere else, to experience an alternative perspective, to have a thrill, to relax. In other words, to become released from fixed or traditional experience. Nakamura describes White performers acting as Asians by replicating stereotypes like the blazing samurai or the seductive geisha. She concludes that, important as it is for unseen faces and unheard voices to appear on the Internet, identity tourism strips the gesture of any potential progressive character, by reducing identity to surface factors and by reducing people to caricature. Needed are both actual and simulated representations of identity on the Internet that fracture rather than consolidate damaging stereotypes. Nakamura writes,

> Programming language and internet connectivity have made it possible for people to interact without putting into play any bodies but the ones they write for themselves. The temporary divorce which cyberdiscourse grants the mind from the body and the text from the body also separates race from the body. Player scripts which eschew repressive versions of the Oriental in favor of critical rearticulations and recombinations of race, gender, and class, and which also call

the fixedness of theses categories into question have the power to turn theatricality characteristics of MOOspace into a true innovative form of play, rather than a tired rearticulation and reinstatement of old hierarchies.[69]

Such racializing of the Internet is no longer confined to the textual world of chat rooms, MUDs, and MOOs (object oriented MUDs). In recent years, the computer gaming industry has introduced a range of non-White characters in releases like *Urban Chaos, Shadow Man, Ready Rumble,* and *Ready 2 Rumble Boxing.* The primarily African American and Asian American figures in these games serve as a relief from the standard White characters that so typified the genre in its emerging years. At the same time, they rearticulate many stereotypes. One might attribute a variety of motives to the introduction of these new games and characters—from a legitimate desire for cultural diversity, to the desire to capture a non-White market share, to the growing suburban White audience for hip-hop culture. Regardless, the fact remains that the game industry appears to be narrowing rather than expanding definitions of what it means to be a person of color.[70]

These disconnections between the often-professed intentions of digital culture (utopian, democratic, universal) and the resulting social consequences (regressive, inegalitarian, exclusionary) remain the central contradiction of this emerging technology. Commenting on the virtual world of computer games and cyberspace, digital apologist Steven Holzman writes in *Digital Mosaics* about what he calls the "virtually real." Decrying the extension of the renaissance obsession with photographic "reality" into computer-generated art and entertainment, Holzman offers what appears to be an antidote: "While the point of these projects is to develop the virtually real, virtual worlds need not be confined to simulations of the real world."[71] This is the crux of "digital aesthetics" in the view of Holzman and numerous other writers—the use of computers to invent new worlds, new experiences, and new realities. As has been discussed throughout this chapter, this age-old dream of a transcendent or idealized virtuality will always be flawed as long as its authors or agents remain tethered to the nonvirtual world. And they always will. The real challenge facing digital culture is to examine the character of that tethering, and to struggle to understand the many reasons that it is ignored, obscured, or denied.

Notes

1. See Richard Coyne, *Technoromanticism: Digital Narrative, Holism, and the Romance of the Real* (Cambridge, Mass.: MIT Press, 1999). Citing Martin Plattel and

others, Coyne presents a detailed discussion of how utopian narratives reflect social anxieties.

2. Jeremy Rifkin, *The Age of Access: The New Culture of Hypercapitalism, Where All of Life Is a Paid-For Experience* (New York: Putnam, 2000), 173.

3. David Rodowick, "Digital Culture: An Uncertain Utopia" (paper presented at the University of California, Irvine, 5 April 1999).

4. Pam Rosenthal, "Jacked In: Fordism, Cyberpunk, Marxism," *Socialist Review*, no. 151 (1991): 79.

5. Paul Virilio, "The Third Interval: A Critical Transition," in *Rethinking Technologies*, ed. Verena Andermatt Conly (Minneapolis: University of Minnesota, 1993), 3.

6. Virilio, "The Third Interval."

7. Bill Gates, *Business@The Speed of Thought* (New York: Time-Warner Books, 1999), 72.

8. Rifkin, *The Age of Access*, 20.

9. Rifkin, *The Age of Access*, 21.

10. Gates, *Business@The Speed of Thought*, 6–7.

11. Marshall McLuhan, *Understanding Media: Extensions of Man* (New York: McGraw Hill, 1964), 23.

12. Marshall McLuhan, as cited in Steven Holzman, *Digital Mosaics: The Aesthetics of Cyberspace* (New York: Touchstone, 1997), 31.

13. Gates, *Business@The Speed of Thought*, 78.

14. Gates, *Business@The Speed of Thought*, 259.

15. Evan Marcus, "The World's First Trillionaire," *Wired* 7.09 (September 1999), 163.

16. Gates announced in 1999 a $1 billion contribution to the United Negro Scholarship Fund, and other minority-oriented educational support groups—and he was harshly criticized by anti-affirmative action conservatives for the nonmeritocratic character of his gift.

17. "Freedom to Innovate Network," http://www.microsoft.com/FREEDOM TOINNOVATE/newsletter/archives.htm [accessed 28 November 1999].

18. United Nations Development Program (UNDP), "Globalization with a Human Face," *Human Development Report 1999* (New York: United Nations Development Report Office, 1999), 3.

19. Gates, *Business@the Speed of Thought*, 297.

20. UNDP, 58.

21. UNDP—all statistics on global technology in this section are from this report.

22. Rifkin, *The Age of Access*, 14.

23. UNDP, 69.

24. Robert McChesney, *Rich Media, Poor Democracy: Communication Politics in Dubious Times* (Chicago: University of Illinois, 1999).

25. Ben J. Bagdikian, *The Media Monopoly*, 4th ed. (Boston: Beacon Press, 1992).

26. Bagdikian, *The Media Monopoly*, 3.

27. Bagdikian, *The Media Monopoly*, 18.

28. Bagdikian, *The Media Monopoly*, 4.

29. Ben J. Bagdikian, interview on *All Things Considered*, National Public Radio, 28 January 2000.

30. McChesney, *Rich Media, Poor Democracy,* 14.

31. McChesney, *Rich Media, Poor Democracy,* 16.

32. Howard Rheingold, *The Virtual Community: Homesteading on the Electronic Frontier* (Addison-Wesley, 1993); Michael Heim, *The Metaphysics of Virtual Reality* (London and New York: Oxford University Press).

33. Howard Rheingold, as quoted in Andrew Calcutt, *White Noise: An A-Z of the Contradictions of Cyberculture* (New York: St Martin's Press, 1999), 29.

34. Michael Heim, as quoted in Ann Travers, *Writing the Public in Cyberspace: Redefining Inclusion on the Net* (New York and London: Garland, 2000), 2.

35. Joe Lockard, "Babel Machines and Electronic Universalism," in *Race in Cyberspace,* ed. Beth E. Kolko, Lisa Nakamura, and Gilbert R. Rodman (New York and London: Routledge, 2000), 178.

36. National Telecommunications and Information Administration (NTIA), *Falling through the Net II: New Data on the Digital Divide* (Washington, D.C.: U.S. Commerce Department, 1999). All statistics in this paragraph come from this report.

37. Donna Hoffman and Thomas Novak, *The Growing Digital Divide: Implications for an Open Research Agenda* (New York: Markle Foundation, 1999), 4.

38. Benton Foundation, *Losing Ground Bit by Bit: Low Income Communities in the Information Age* (Washington, D.C.: Benton Foundation, 1999), 4. See also Beth E. Kolko, Lisa Nakamura, and Gilbert R. Rodman, eds., *Race in Cyberspace* (London and New York: Routledge, 2000); Peter Lunenfeld, *Snap to Grid: A User's Guide to Digital Arts, Media, and Cultures* (Cambridge, Mass.: MIT Press, 2000); Michael Margolis and David Resnick, *Politics as Usual: The Cyberspace "Revolution"* (Thousand Oaks, Calif.: Sage, 2000); Ann Travers, *Writing the Public in Cyberspace: Redefining Inclusion on the Net* (London and New York: Garland Publishing, 2000).

39. Benton Foundation, *Losing Ground Bit by Bit,* 7.

40. Educational Testing Service, "Computers and Classrooms: The Status of Technology in U.S. Schools" (Princeton, N.J.: Educational Testing Service, 1999).

41. Educational Testing Service, "Computers and Classrooms."

42. Benton Foundation, *Losing Ground Bit by Bit,* iv.

43. Benton Foundation, "Losing Ground Bit by Bit: Low Income Communities in the Information Age," http://benton.org/library/low-income/home.html [accessed 28 November 1999].

44. U.S. Department of Commerce, "Falling through the Net: Defining the Digital Divide," http://www.ntia.doc.gov/ntiahome/fttn99/contents/html [accessed 20 July 2000].

45. Stanley Aronowitz, "Technology and the Future of Work," in *Cultures on the Brink,* ed. Timothy Druckrey (Seattle: Bay Press, 1994), 15.

46. Aronowitz, "Technology and the Future of Work," 20.

47. Rifkin, *The Age of Access,* 125.

48. U.S. Commerce Department, *America's New Deficit: The Shortage of Information Technology Workers* (Washington, D.C.: U.S. Commerce Department, 1999).

49. Bureau of Labor Statistics, *The Employment Situation: October 1999* (Washington, D.C.: U.S. Commerce Department, 1999), 1.

50. As cited in Paulina Borsook, *Cyberselfish: A Critical Romp Through the Terribly Libertarian Culture of High Tech* (New York: Public Affairs, 2000), 174.

51. David Bolt and Ray Crawford, *The Digital Divide: Computers and Our Children's Future* (New York: TV Books, 2000), 117.

52. Guillermo Gómez-Peña, "The Virtual Barrio@the Other Frontier," in *Clicking In: Hot Links to a Digital Culture,* ed. Lynn Hershman Leeson (Seattle: Bay Press, 1996), 176.

53. John Ogbu, as cited in Tamar Jacoby, "Color Blind: The African American Absence in High Tech," *The New Republic* 220, no. 13 (29 March 1999): 25.

54. Ogbu, in Jacoby, "Color Blind," 25.

55. Chris O'Mally, "The Digital Divide," *Time*, 22 March 1999, 86.

56. William Gibson, *Burning Chrome* (New York: Ace Books, 1986), 170.

57. Jean Lave and Jane Wenger, as quoted in Ann Travers, *Writing the Public in Cyberspace: Redefining Inclusion on the Net* (New York and London: Garland, 2000), 19.

58. See Nelly Oudshoorn, "A Natural Order of Things: Reproductive Science and the Politics of Othering," in *Future Natural: Nature/Science/Culture,* ed. George Robertson et al. (New York and London: Routledge, 1996).

59. Barbara Katz Rothman, as cited in Robbie Davis-Floyd and Joseph Dumit, eds., *Cyborg Babies: From Techno-Sex to Techno-Tots* (New York and London: Routledge, 1998), 3.

60. Stanley Aronowitz, *Science as Power: Discourse and Ideology in Modern Society* (Minneapolis: University of Minnesota, 1988), x. See also Ken Goldberg, ed., *The Robot in the Garden: Telerobotics and Telepistemology in the Age of the Internet* (Cambridge, Mass.: MIT Press, 2000). Gill Kirkup et al., eds., *The Gendered Cyborg: A Reader* (London and New York: Routledge, 2000).

61. Sandra Harding, *Is Science Multicultural? Postcolonialisms, Feminisms, Epistemologies* (Bloomington and Indianapolis: University of Indiana, 1998), 7.

62. Harding, *Is Science Multicultural?*, 7.

63. Cameron Bailey, "Virtual Skin: Articulating Race in Cyberspace," in *Immersed in Technology: Art and Virtual Environments,* ed. Anne Moser and Douglas (Cambridge: MIT, 1996), 38.

64. Joseph Lockard, "Progressive Politics, Electronic Individualism, and the Myth of the Virtual Community," in *Internet Culture,* ed. David Porter (New York and London: Routledge, 1997), 227.

65. Lockard, "Progressive Politics."

66. Sherry Turkle, *Life on the Screen: Identity in the Age of the Internet* (New York: Touchstone, 1995), 15. See also: Stephanie Gibson and Ollie Oviedo, eds., *The Emerging Cyberculture: Literacy, Paradigm, and Paradox* (Cresskill, N.J.: Hampton Press, 2000).

67. Beth E. Kolko, Lisa Nakamura, and Gilbert R. Rodman, eds., *Race in Cyberspace* (New York and London: Routledge, 2000).

68. Robyn Weigman, *American Anatomies: Theorizing Race and Gender* (Durham, N.C.: Duke, 1995), 21. The residue of purportedly scientific theories of race is considered in some depth in Sarah E. Chin, *Technology and the Logic of American Racism* (New York: Continuum, 2000).

69. Lisa Nakamura, "Race in/for Cyberspace: Identity Tourism and Racial Passing on the Internet," *Works and Days: Essays in the Socio-Historical Dimensions of Litera-*

ture and the Arts 13 nos. 1–2 (Spring–Fall 1995), 181. A later version appears in Beth E. Kolko, Lisa Nakamura, and Gilbert R. Rodman, eds., *Race in Cyberspace*, 15–27.

70. Michael Marriot, "Blood, Gore, Sex and Now: Race," *New York Times* (21 October 1999), D1, 7.

71. Steven Holzman, *Digital Mosaics: The Aesthetics of Cyberspace* (New York: Touchstone, 1997), 45. See also Lunenfeld, *Snap to Grid*.

3

The Education Business

TREMENDOUS CHANGES have taken place in education during the past decade—changes that have laid the groundwork for a radical technological transformation of schools in the coming years. As the "tidal wave" of baby boomers' children moves from elementary school to college levels, the digital mechanization of teaching is moving at a quick pace. But the introduction of technology into the nation's schools and universities could never have been imagined unless a fundamental transformation had occurred in the way education was organized, managed, and funded. It took the introduction of corporations into education to get the job done.

A confluence of several cultural, political, and economic factors made this transformation of education possible. The back-to-basics reform movements of the 1980s, rooted as they were in the liberal/conservative culture wars, concerned themselves largely with the content of education: the books, courses, teaching methods, school regulations, and values that made up the educational experience. With the ascent of Bill Clinton to the White House, the culture wars continued to be fought over issues ranging from the arts and entertainment to the personal behavior of public figures. But in education they went underground, leaving behind a residue of public discontent and suspicion that enabled structural changes in schools at local, state, and federal levels. Meanwhile, as college moved from an option to a career necessity for entrance into the middle class, pressure grew to control skyrocketing tuition—as new demands were placed on colleges to broaden the kind of education they delivered. As a result, institutions of higher learning began to change how they operated, often at the expense of their more traditional functions.

The economic context for these changes is significant. During the 1990s the number and magnitude of corporate mergers reached unprecedented levels. By the end of the decade, yearly mergers had topped $1 trillion—a 50 percent increase over their 1996 level.[1] As America Online merged with Time–Warner, MCI bought Sprint, Daimler–Benz bought Chrysler, and Westinghouse acquired CBS. With the so-called triumph of capitalism across the globe and the relaxation of international trade barriers, multinational corporations grew and prospered as never before. Meanwhile within the United States, government budget surpluses and the meteoric rise of the stock market fueled a media-driven belief that the booming economy could never go bust. On many levels it seemed that the enlightened corporation was the engine of utopia.

Always a politicized activity, education functioned in the nation's first 150 years as an instrument of assimilation, normalization, and class stratification. Its meritocratic reward structure reinforced the desire of an increasingly industrialized society for workplace conformity and productivity. As the United States advanced to its role as an international superpower, schools were regarded as a source of burgeoning military and economic strength. This was reflected in the massive resources committed to science education and research during the Cold War years. Such an instrumental view of schooling still drives most educational policy debates.

It should come as no surprise that as computer technology and Internet stocks captured the nation's imagination at the end of the 1990s, these values would be mapped onto education. But unlike past technological revolutions, the digital age has been driven by the very institution that high-speed communication has helped to bring into existence: the multinational corporation. The result has been a transformation of education to an unprecedented, yet largely underacknowledged, extent. As the public has been treated to an endless repetition of emotional debates over vouchers, school uniforms, and prayer at football games, the unquestioned value of technology in education has opened the door to myriad commercial enterprises, their methods of operation, and the underlying ideologies that motivate them.

Everything Old Is New Again

Setting the stage for the corporatization of education was a long and largely successful assault on progressive school policies initiated in the Reagan/Bush years and carried on during the Clinton presidency. For much of the past two decades the conservative reform movement has set the tone for educational policy in the United States. With the economic downturns of the 1970s and 1980s, supply-side analysts blamed schools for the nation's inability to compete in world markets—while, ironically, arguing for reductions in federal education spending. This resulted in intensified intervention in the form of curriculum changes, corporate management techniques, and a philosophy reoriented toward social reproduction and worker preparation. A renewed emphasis was placed on course content—specifically content that would reinforce traditional "values." As Lynne V. Cheney argued, the biggest "culprit is 'process'—the belief that we can teach our children how to think without troubling them to learn anything worth thinking about."[2]

The approach to schooling touted by reformers offers a model of an unchanging social order that perpetuates existing hierarchies of power and privilege. This program of education reform reintroduces bureaucratic control, measurement, and ranking in the service of a capital-driven curriculum of basic skills. It promotes an unquestioning view of authority and cultural heritage. As such it represents the antithesis of a pluralistic democracy, focusing instead on techniques of social stratification and discrimination. As discussed a decade ago by Samuel Lipman:

> What is necessary are definitions of culture and democracy based less on the muddling of definitions and more on their clarification, less on inclusions and more on exclusions, less on finding similarities between conflicting realities, concepts, and goals and more on recognizing the differences between them.[3]

This philosophy of social stratification extended beyond the realm of ideas. Throughout the Reagan and Bush years, federal support for education fell, despite much pro-family, pro-education rhetoric. With the ultimate goal of eliminating the U.S. Department of Education and privatizing as many public institutions as possible, conservative politicians enacted budget cuts that greatly compromised the federal government's role as an economic equalizer among school districts. Throughout the 1980s the gap widened dramatically between rich and poor schools, creating a divide that only intensified with the corporate invasion of the 1990s.

At first merchandise vendors and technology companies viewed schools as markets—the more upscale the school the better. This phenomenon made news when Christopher Whittle's Channel One was introduced to K–12 education. In exchange for audiovisual and computer equipment, schools agreed to require students to watch a daily "news" segment with Pepsi and Nike "commercials." Channel One is now seen by 40 percent of U.S. students. The trend has continued, with school districts permitting promotional materials on buses and in corridors and textbooks. Further, fast-food companies such as Taco Bell and Wendy's have taken over cafeteria franchises.

"Underfunded schools, desperate for resources, are increasingly receptive to corporate-sponsored educational materials and programs, and are ever more accepting of the associated commercialism and product promotion," observed Peggy Charren of the advocacy group Action for Children's Television.[4] Recent examples are truly disturbing. In Jefferson County, Colorado, Pepsi gained the exclusive right to market its products in 140 schools by donating $2 million to build a high school stadium. Elsewhere third-graders learn math by counting Tootsie Rolls and older students study business by viewing materials about how a McDonald's restaurant is run.[5] All in all, the educational investment firm EdVentures estimates the market in schools at between $630 billion and $680 billion. *Our Children* magazine identifies four fundamental categories of in-school commercialism:

In-school ads: book covers, wall advertisements, billboards, telephone kiosks, audio advertisements on public address systems, and give-away products or coupons.

Ads in classroom materials or programs: Channel One and similar audio, video, or print-media material that mix curricular content with commercial content.

Sponsored educational materials: curricular materials or supplementary audio, visual, or printed items that favor or mention a commercial producer.

Corporate-sponsored contests or incentive programs: offering prizes or sponsoring events featuring students who excel in a particular area while promoting a product or corporation.[6]

Tenured Radicals and Other Fictions

Business entered the university in a different way. On college campuses the ground was laid for a corporate takeover by a calculated campaign to discredit the way the university operated. Funded during the 1980s and 1990s by conservative corporations, foundations, and think tanks was an endless barrage of new reports, editorials, journal articles, and books about the purported control of higher education by the left. Despite the brouhaha on college campuses about political correctness, speech codes, literary canons, multiculturalism, and intellectual freedom of expression, many conservatives now admit that the left presents little real threat in the academy. After nearly a decade of media hysteria over the presumed subversion of "tenured radicals" and leftist "thought police," the credibility of such assertions is wearing thin. As free-market apologist David Rieff wrote in *Harper's*, "Radicals on campus are no more dangerous than a display of Mao caps and jackets would be in Bloomingdales." Moreover, the ranks of the enemy turn out to be much smaller than advertised.

In a recent survey of college professors conducted by the Carnegie Foundation for the Advancement of Teaching, when given a choice from among five labels to describe themselves (left, liberal, middle-of-the-road, moderately conservative, and strongly conservative) a mere 5.8 percent described themselves as "left" and only 33.8 percent as "liberal."[7] These statistics suggest that the danger of radicals on campus may be more of an illusion than an imminent catastrophe. Another more subtle indication of the ideological climate in academic circles can be determined from what scholars are reading. A recent study conducted by Steven Brint indicated that the following constitute the ten "most influential periodicals among American intellectuals": *New York Review of Books, New Republic, New York Times Book Review, Foreign Affairs, Commentary, Atlantic Monthly, New Yorker, Public Interest, National Review,* and *New Criterion*.[8]

When it comes to publishing political journals, conservative money talks. As reported in *Extra!*, the monthly publication of Fairness and Accuracy in Media, the right has far outspent the left in supporting periodicals. During the 1990s, right-wing foundations invested $2.7 million in four conservative publications: *New Criterion, National Interest, Public Interest,* and *American Spectator*. In contrast, during the same period left-wing foundations invested just 10 percent of that amount—$269,000—in *The Nation, The Progressive, Mother Jones,* and *In These Times*.[9]

Actually, the fear of a leftist menace in the academy has a contemporary history dating to the communist witch hunts of the McCarthy era. These anxieties surfaced again in a more subtle form in the 1980s, when the right started to mobilize against a perceived crisis in the humanities. With the ascent of Ronald Reagan to the White House, conservatives launched a governmentally sanctioned reform program. Resentful of the social changes of the 1960s and 1970s, administration appointees such as William J. Bennett (then-chair of the National Endowment for the Humanities) and T. E. Bell (secretary of education) issued calls to "reclaim a legacy" and to attend to a "nation at risk."[10] These efforts fueled concerns within higher education over the challenges posed to traditional regimes of knowledge from new interdisciplinary areas like ethnic studies, media studies, and women's studies.

A trickle-down effect to public schools soon followed. In K–12 education, conservative reformers called for an end to what were called "cafeteria style" course offerings like social studies and current events—and a return to a basic curriculum of core courses.[11] Such curricular critiques were part of a broader program to discredit the very concept of a public system of education, which conservatives claimed had lost touch with mainstream values and had inappropriately "overeducated" certain segments of the workforce.[12] Thus began a twelve-year initiative to privatize the nation's schools—an effort that culminated in "education president" George H. W. Bush's infamous "America 2000" reform plan.[13] Perhaps not so surprisingly, Bill Clinton appropriated large portions of the Bush agenda into his own "Goals 2000" education initiative of standardized core curricula and national achievement tests. Although it lacked the free-market zeal of Bush's scheme of government vouchers to encourage the abandonment of public schools, it shared a pro-business emphasis on competition, hierarchical reward structures, and "world-class standards."[14]

Central to this corporatist agenda has been a systematic depoliticization of formerly public areas of civic life. Evoking the crude logic that government erodes individual liberty and choice, arguments are made for the privatization of education, communication, and culture—in effect, placing such policy issues beyond the reach of the electorate. To rationalize these efforts, conservatives accused leftists of using such public institutions as education to indoctrinate unsuspecting young people. Efforts by women, people of color, lesbians, gay men, students, the disabled, and other groups to gain admission to campuses or effect curricular changes were labeled partisan incursions into a realm of otherwise detached scholarship.

Aggravating these tensions were the questions posed by postmodernism to the foundational truths on which so many scholarly institutions were founded. Proponents of these views were characterized as placing "the academy under siege by leftists, multiculturalists, deconstructionists, and other radicals who are politicizing the university and threatening to undermine the very foundations of Western intellectual traditions."[15] Political correctness similarly was branded a national blight, or more ominously as the first indication of a creeping socialism. Writing in *Newsweek* Jerry Adler admonished that there are many "who recognize the tyranny of PC, but see it only as a transitional phase, which will no longer be necessary once the virtues of tolerance are internalized. Does that sound familiar? It's the dictatorship of the proletariat."[16]

This nervousness over the purported ideological "pollution" of the academy became manifest in titles of books like Roger Kimball's *Tenured Radicals: How Politics Has Corrupted Higher Education* and Dinesh D'Sousa's *Illiberal Education: The Politics of Race and Sex on Campus.*[17] Rather than treating changes on university campuses as the healthy outgrowth of collegial debate, writers like Kimball and D'Sousa blamed them for ills ranging from the decline in national productivity to the rise in urban violence. To Kimball in particular, the incursion of campus leftists constituted nothing less than an absolute takeover of higher education:

Far from being the work of a besieged minority, these voices represent the new academic establishment of tenured radicals. Often they are among the most highly paid professors—those for whose services our leading universities bid against each other in little-publicized auctions. Nor is the influence of these professors confined to the present moment. At many prestigious institutions they are precisely the people helping to shape the future by making faculty appointments, overseeing promotions, and devising the educational program in the humanities—efforts at self-propagation that virtually ensure their continued domination for another generation.[18]

This suspicion over the politicization of learning has very old roots in the Cartesian distancing of intellect from material existence. Within this logic the subjective pursuits of the mind are strictly separated from the dispassionate rules by which society is governed. This disinterestedness is said to emerge from a common respect for universal principles that lie beyond human challenge or revision. Education functions to preserve these traditions by transmitting them to future generations. As D'Sousa put it,

> The liberal university is a distinctive and fragile institution. It is not an all-purpose instrument of social change. Its function is indeed to serve the larger society which supports and sustains it, yet it does not best do this when it makes itself indistinguishable from the helter-skelter of pressure politics.[19]

By the early 1990s these arguments began to surface outside the academy, as politicians and religious personalities like Alfonse D. Amato, Patrick Buchanan, the Rev. Jerry Falwell, Jesse Helms, Dan Quayle, and the Rev. Pat Robertson sought to cash in on the political capital to be gained by scapegoating radical academics. Evoking a reactionary populism to capitalize on the distance of intellectuals from the average citizen, conservatives successfully constructed the specter of a left-wing "thought police."[20] Meanwhile, within colleges and universities, the right began mobilizing its own backlash with the organization of "young conservative" student groups and faculty associations like the National Association of Scholars.

What limited gains the left had made in the ensuing culture wars quickly began to erode. In all fairness, many proponents of political correctness *were* former socialists, but very few of them were making the sort of broad-based assaults on higher education they were accused of committing. Nevertheless, from presidential addresses to cover stories on publications like *Time* and *Newsweek* the public was inundated with accounts of a "new McCarthyism" on campuses inflicted by the left wing. At the center of the hoopla was the ironic assertion that the political correctness had itself become a tyrannizing practice, threatening to silence all who would dare to dissent. Rosa Ehrenreich counters such charges of academic piracy with the comment:

A national survey of college administrators released last summer found that "political correctness" is not the campus issue it has been portrayed to be by pundits and politicians of the political right. . . . According to the survey's findings, faculty members complained of pressure from students and fellow professors to alter the political and cultural content of their courses at only 5 percent of all colleges. So much for the influence of radicals, tenured or otherwise.[21]

Within a short time, proponents of diversity and deconstruction were alternating between damage control and self-reassurance. Speaking of what small progressive advances had been made, Gregory Jay observed, "Judged by an absolute standard, these successes may seem pathetic, but in the practical world of everyday struggle they deserve our support," adding that "today's institutions of higher learning remain dominated by traditional groups and ideologies that perpetuate misrepresentation. It's true."[22] The overall impact of what has been termed "the mugging of the academic left" has been a further marginalization of radical educators and a generalized chilling of free speech on campuses. What began as a series of progressive movements to open the university to formerly excluded voices ended as an excuse for extremists and demagogues to further reduce such possibilities.

How did this misunderstanding come about? By some accounts, the scapegoating of the academic left is a result of its ghettoization within the university. Following World War II, two significant changes in the job market left radical intellectuals with little choice but to become college professors.[23] The first was the much-lamented decline in "little magazines" that provided publishing outlets—and a modest source of income—for a range of "public intellectuals" on both sides of the political spectrum. This impingement on the livelihood and the sense of community among scholars coincided neatly with educational demands of the GI Bill and postwar baby boom. Aided by a massive influx of federal money through such subsequent measures as the 1958 National Defense Education Act (which for the first time gave direct aid to nonveterans), colleges and their professorates grew at a staggering pace. At the close of the 1960s, the number of graduate students had become greater than that of undergraduates in 1940. By the late 1980s, the number of colleges and universities would double and the overall number of students would grow by 800 percent.[24] As a result the university became a vocational centrifuge for intellectuals of all political stripes—that is, until the rise of privately funded, nonuniversity conservative think tanks in the Reagan years.

Once committed to the gulag of the ivory tower, the academic left's ability for popular communication soon atrophied. In part this estrangement from "the people" grew from a simple de-skilling. Experts at such discursive forms as the graduate seminar, the grant application, or the arcane footnote found themselves at a loss in the strange context of the network sound bite or the newspaper op-ed page.[25] Such is the natural consequence of working in an atmosphere in which obscure specialization is the norm and esoteric language the rule. Finally the estrangement of the academic progressives from mainstream culture resulted from a genuine contempt for it. The development of these attitudes during the 1960s and 1970s will be discussed at length in the next chapter. Of importance here is the extent to which liberal groups have abandoned popular culture—especially the mass media—in their political theorizing. No wonder radicals have found themselves with a public relations problem.

The small contingents of progressives that have made forays into the popular realm are villainized, often in racial terms. Serious thinkers from communities of color have made consistent efforts to bridge the popular/elite divide. Partly motivated by the historic exclusions of the academy, writers like Michael Dyson, Richard Rodriguez, Lani Guinier, Gayatri Spivak, Edward Said, Toni Morrison, and Vine Deloria have successfully established themselves as "public intellectuals." In the mid-1990s a rash of reactionary press accounts—focusing primarily on writing by African American scholars—began to discuss this phenomenon in the pages of periodicals like *New Republic, Atlantic Monthly, New Yorker,* and *Village Voice.* In the most benign instances, these articles treated the successes of certain figures as historical anomalies created by an insurgent politics of identity. In their more pernicious forms these stories have conveyed a thinly veiled contempt. The latter view is exemplified by Leon Wieseltier's much-discussed condemnation of Cornel West in the *New Republic,* an essay long on rhetoric and short on substance. Wieseltier contends that "since there is no crisis in America more insurgent than the crisis of race, and since there is no intellectual in America more celebrated for his consideration of race, I turned to West, and read his books. They are almost completely useless."[26] This is not to suggest that West is beyond criticism, or even that he is in need of criticism due to the timidness of a liberal press. However, as Salim Mukakkil has suggested, this quick condemnation of the new public intellectuals has coincidentally arrived at exactly the point when their ranks are no longer a White preserve. To Mukakkil:

> The addition of the word "public" to any institution instantly devalues it in our current cultural iconography: public schools, public pools, public transportation, public hospitals. These institutions are devalued in part because they are associated with minorities. In that sense, the rise of the black public intellectuals may represent less than it seems.[27]

The Corporate University

In the late 1990s this disdain for things "public" found a lightning rod in higher education, where during the past decade governance, instruction, and research had been increasingly privatized to emulate the function of the corporation. These changes became manifest early in the decade in administrative hiring trends, as growing numbers of college and university presidents were recruited, not from the ranks of the professorate as had traditionally been the case, but from the business community. In a report titled "Renewing the Academic Presidency," the Association of Governing Boards recommended the recruitment of presidents from outside the academy to ensure that selected individuals possessed sufficient expertise in such areas as personnel, budgeting, and fund-raising—not to mention the all-important skills of communicating and negotiating with business people. What began as a simple emphasis on efficiency and productivity within the university evolved into prejudice toward leaders from inside schools: what Brother Patrick Ellis calls the "faculty as problem" attitude.[28] Presidents that are chosen from within the academy are now more likely to be drawn from business schools, as is the case with Cornell's Alan Merton, Tulane's Scott Cowen, and University of Texas Chancellor William Cunningham—along with nearly a dozen other appointees in recent years.[29]

These changes at the top are perhaps the least publicized manifestation of the growing reorientation of university hiring and personnel policies. Even as student applications steadily increased and the aging cohort of post-World War II faculty reached retirement age in the 1990s, university budgets and numbers of tenure-track appointments continued to decrease steadily. This was done to maximize the university's efficiency and to maintain maximum flexibility for its administration. Cary Nelson explains,

As universities struggle with increasingly constrained budgets, the temptation to make ends meet by exploiting more vulnerable employees grows daily. Industry meanwhile provides a handbook of relevant strategies and techniques: make paying workers as little as possible a basic managerial principle and goal; deny employee benefits any time you can get away with it; disguise your responsibilities for the most abused workers by subcontracting for their services; during contract negotiations offer nothing until frustration peaks, then make generous salary and job security offers to long term employees on the condition that they agree to decrease their numbers through attrition; establish multiple tiers of compensation, hiring all new employees on substantially lower salaries . . . minimize what different classes of employees know about each other's compensation; promote an ideology of loyalty, dedication, and service dependent on self-denial.[30]

In institution after institution, full-time professors were replaced by part-time instructors, as graduate assistants increasingly shouldered heavier responsibilities in the classroom. The 1996 strikes at Yale and the City University of New York, and the 1999 unionization of graduate students in the University of California system, were but two indications of the crisis facing academic labor at the end of the decade. Writing in the *New Republic*, Michael Walzer characterizes the situation by stating,

> An increasing proportion of undergraduate teaching is done by adjuncts and assistants of various kinds, who work on short-term contracts and cannot be expected to have normal academic careers. It is now possible to imagine an economy in which the American workforce will be divided into a full-time elite and a large number of harried, unhappy and exploited workers rushing from one part-time job or temporary job to another, always insecure, barely able to make ends meet. . . . Maximum efficiency requires, so the world was told in 1840 and again in 1997, though not in so many words, disposable workers—men and women who will work long hours or short, "as necessary," and disappear without complaint when the necessities change.[31]

While this proletarianization of academic labor was taking place, corporations were also partnering with universities to privatize a variety of institutional services. As a result student union buildings and cafeterias took on the appearance—or were conceptualized from the beginning—as shopping malls or food courts, as vendors competed to place university logos on caps, mugs, and credit cards. This is part of a larger pattern in what has been termed the "Disneyfication" of college life. As Kevin Robbins and Frank Webster explain, a pervasive impulse toward infotainment has emerged with the university in Disney fashion, "where learning is 'fun,' the staff 'perky,' where consumer considerations dictate the curriculum, where presentation takes precedence over substance, and where students are 'consumers.' "[32]

More serious has been the growing role of corporations in curriculum. Schools across the nation are offering up new buildings (or in a few instances, entire campuses) as philanthropic "naming opportunities" and endowed professorships as advertisements for whoever will put up the cash. The University of California at Irvine recently announced the nation's first Taco Bell Chair of Business Administration. The businesslike drive in university management is giving way to courses and academic programs to serve the needs of corporations. More and more universities are yielding either to the direct demands of employers seeking vocationally trained applicants or to indirect pressures that they become more "community oriented" or "less elitist" in what they offer. This is occurring in an environment in which public universities and community colleges are struggling to compete with a growing number of for-profit vocational schools like ITT and Heald Technical Colleges, as well as expanding commercial academic/vocational hybrids like the University of Phoenix that operate largely on the Internet.

Meanwhile, fewer and fewer students value the traditional liberal arts or general education that prepared prior generations of college students with skills of communication, critical reasoning, or humanistic awareness. They respect only what is applicable to the job market. Currently less than 25 percent of students nationwide are enrolled in liberal arts programs. Of the remaining students, nearly one-third are in business programs, with the others studying in career-related fields like health care or teaching.[33] Eleven percent of bachelor's degrees are awarded in the social sciences and history, 3 percent in the humanities, and 1 percent in foreign languages. The American Council on Higher Education reports that more than 50 percent of students select colleges where "graduates get good jobs" and 75 percent said that "it is essential or very important to be well off financially."[34] Although 60 percent indicated that gaining "a general education and appreciation of ideas" is an important reason to go to school, many indicated that they assumed this would occur through the study of business. What is behind this heightened pragmatism? Although pessimists invariably fault the character of the current generation of students, the more likely answer is that college has simply become more important in vocational terms. No longer an "optional" holding tank to instill young people with humanistic values through their transition to adulthood, a college degree—and the *right* college degree—is now seen as essential for a good job. As a consequence students have become critical educational consumers—with all of the negative and positive characteristics that this implies.

This pressure is coming from student populations at a time when many administrators are urging staff members and faculty to view students, as discussed earlier, less as a captive audience of subordinates and more as "customers" or "clients." Unfortunately, the drive to satisfy these clients is occurring when the general level of student preparedness for college is dropping. As test scores of entering students continue to decline and remediation needs for basic language skills increase, approximately 75 percent of first-year students fail to return as sophomores and half of those who do return do not complete their degrees.[35]

The reasons for this level of failure are complex. Among other things, the situation can be seen as a result of rising child poverty rates, inadequate preschool and K–12 funding, growing immigrant and non-English-speaking populations, and an increased shortage of qualified elementary and secondary school teachers. Yet rather than addressing these serious structural problems, the commonsense answer advanced by conservative ideologues—which regrettably is broadcast in the popular media—is that the character of young people is declining and along with it their willingness to work hard in school. Columnist George Will cites a growing "student incivility" reflected in "coming to classes late and leaving early, eating, conversing, reading newspapers, talking on cell phones, sleeping, watching portable televisions and directing verbal abuse at teachers."[36] Will concludes that "there are simply too many students who have neither the aptitude nor the attitudes that should be prerequisites for going to college."[37]

Hardly an isolated opinion, this contempt for college students is emblematic of an underlying dislike of higher education among conservatives—or more precisely, a dislike of *public* higher education. In part, these attitudes stem from memories of student political activism in the 1960s, when college campuses were seen as incubators for radical anti-American sentiments—not to mention the contemporary feminist, Black-power, Chicano, and gay-rights movements. During this period, student movements successfully challenged prevailing regimes of social reproduction, demonstrating that the new generation was no longer uniformly loyal to the politics and values of pre-World War II America. Challenging foreign policy, domestic inequity, capitalist greed, and ecological devastation, the 1960s student movements constituted the first internal threat to the "military-industrial complex" that the nation had seen since the socialist and communist movements of the 1930s.

The negative attitudes toward public universities also derive from traditional alarmist attitudes toward young people in general—the fabrication of what Mike Males has termed the "scapegoat generation."[38] From James Dean to Easy-E, adolescent alienation has made good editorial copy to inflame the anxieties of the middle-aged and the middle and upper classes. Reading news accounts about youthful laziness, promiscuity, and criminality—one gets the idea that the current generation of youth is bankrupt of social concern, political commitment, or capacity for action, aside from an occasional schoolyard mass murder. These perceptions are far from accurate, yet they reflect the all-too-familiar capacities of mass media to homogenize social groups into artificial totalities and to demonize those that are not easily understood. If the current generation does indeed have a unique identity, perhaps it lies in the degree to which it has been written about and labeled. Andrew Ross has commented that the 1990s marked a time when "with the cessation of Cold War antagonisms and an uneasy interregnum in effect, the full force of media punditry had come to be trained on the new postboomer sensibilities. Youth, in this context, would be analyzed as a symptom of this or that prophetic comment about the near future."[39]

The assault on public education also reflects the budgetary and enrollment difficulties of private colleges and universities, which have become too expensive for middle- and working-class families, and now often lose the best students to public institutions. These sentiments are typified in reports like the Cato Institute's "The Threat to Independent Education: Public Subsidies and Private Colleges." Arguing that "private colleges are essential to diverse and independent education and to the maintenance of a civil society independent of the state," the report documents the changes in college education from the beginning of the twentieth century (when 80 percent of college students attended private schools) to the end of the century (when 80 percent attend public institutions).[40] Such nostalgia is hardly accidental, for the hidden agenda of such thinking is indeed a return to days of college as an elite and exclusive institution—free, for the most part, of women, minorities, immigrants, or the poor. In this sense, the anti-public education program represents a generalized assault on education as a social force, inasmuch as public institutions encourage working-class or disempowered citizens to imagine a future beyond the status quo. Within this logic, an "overeducated" working class is a "destabilizing" force and should be reduced to whatever extent is possible.[41]

In many ways these debates over colleges and universities constitute little more than extensions of larger arguments about the role of education as a social technology. Historically liberals have tended to view education as a "corrective" institution that works toward leveling social inequities. Conservatives have favored a meritocratic view in which education supports achievement and social stratification. The way higher education actually functions is a combination of these two approaches. Stanley Aronowitz states that since World War II, higher-education institutions have arranged themselves in a loose, yet hierarchically tiered, formation. At the top are research universities, which primarily produce "new knowledge" in the service of social and economic interests.[42] The second tier is composed mostly of liberal arts and technical colleges, whose primary function is to transmit the knowledge produced in the higher-tier research universities. The third tier represents community colleges and other two-year business and vocational schools. Although viewed by some as stepping-stones to tier-one or tier-two institutions, tier three is increasingly a terminal point for people who will work technical jobs in business and industry. Also, "given the shrinking demand for technical workers of all kinds, the community college is increasingly important as an ideological institution insofar as it fulfills, but only in the bureaucratic sense, the promise of higher education for all."[43]

Before the 1980s, tier-one research universities operated with a relatively heterogeneous array of funding sources—government agencies, foundations, corporations, individual contributors—in producing new knowledge often for its own sake, or without an immediate use. The largest share of money came from the Pentagon because the federal government recognized the generalized importance of research—including the necessity of occasionally funding failed projects—for the long-term interest of the nation. With the economic crises of the 1980s and the ideologically driven cuts to public institutions of all kinds, the character of research began to change. Corporations were needed to fill the funding void, and they did—but at a cost.

Intellectual Capital

By the 1990s, university research nearly had been transformed into a completely privately sponsored affair, driven by the rapidly growing and hugely profitable industries in bioscience and information technology. In this environment any notions of "pure" science or speculative research took a backseat to projects that could produce new drugs, genetically engineered cotton, or a faster microprocessing chip. The moral implications of this are profound, considering the effects of multinational capital on scientific inequity. To take the pharmaceutical industry as just one example, the overwhelming majority of research investment in the past decade has gone not to saving the lives of millions of people in the developing world, but to what have been called "lifestyle drugs" for such maladies as impotence, obesity, baldness, and wrinkles. Long thought to have been nearly eliminated in modern history, new resistant strains of malaria, tuberculosis, and the respiratory infections killed 6.1 million people last year.[44] Yet of the 1,223 new medications introduced during that period, only 13 (or 1 percent) were developed for those illnesses. The Pharmaceutical Research and Manufacturers of America reports that $24 billion will be spent on research for new drugs next year and that the average new medication costs $500 million. But the payoffs can be rewarding—with Viagra sales reported by Pfizer to total more than $1 billion in its first year alone. By contrast, total global expenditures for malaria treatment stand at $84 million, with a total of $2 billion projected to be expended during the next twenty years—a period during which the disease will kill 40 million Africans alone. This is what happens when profits dictate research agendas.

Across the nation universities are slowly succumbing to this corporate agenda. In the new commercial environment where product research and patent development are the primary functions of university scholarship, the fundamental purpose of the university is changing: no longer pursuing knowledge for its own sake, or intellectual experimentation for the common good, but knowledge as a commercial product. Increasingly researchers and other intellectuals who can produce new knowledge run the risk of becoming little more than twenty-first-century factory laborers. Meanwhile, the civic function of the university as a forum for "disinterested" inquiry is disintegrating, and along with it a healthy measure of public trust the institution once held.

Faculty are doing little to change matters. For some this is due to their own complicity in the knowledge factory. Successful researchers are no longer supported merely by grants or fellowships. Those affiliated with companies like Lucent Technologies, Cisco Systems, or Texas Instruments stand to make millions in licensing agreements or stock options. Annual surveys by the Association of University Technology Managers indicate that license revenues at participating universities grew by 20 percent between 1991 and 1996, and an additional 33 percent by 1998. The latest such survey shows that 132 universities share approximately $300 million in such revenues, with the University of California system accounting for a whopping 20 percent of the money.[45] Admittedly, this kind of return is available only to a fortunate few researchers. Of the remaining faculty, a large number are silenced by a growing fear of losing their jobs or guilt about tenure. As academic work has been shifted to part-time, temporary instructors, faculty with lifetime employment contracts have grown sheepish. Few recognize the importance—the necessity—of extending solidarity to lecturers or graduate teaching assistants.

Today the university—like school in general—is feeling pressure on numerous fronts to change in other fundamental ways. Students are more pragmatic and demanding of a curriculum that can deliver concrete material returns, college administrators feel obliged to become more businesslike and efficient, voters and legislators remain distrustful of the ability of schools and colleges to manage themselves, corporations see education as both a marketplace and source of new items to market, and all of these parties argue that free enterprise and competition should be the engines that propel schools into the twenty-first century. And the stakes are growing. The extraordinary attention colleges are receiving derives from the growing recognition of the university as a driving force of the information economy as marketplace, as producer of knowledge capital, and as workforce trainer.

Obviously much gets lost in this formulation. In a recent article in the *Chronicle of Higher Education*, Michael Bérubé responds to a section of Newt Gingrich's book *To Renew America* in which Gingrich suggests that universities should be run like the automobile industry.

> Let's imagine what American universities would be like if they were run like car companies. University CEOs would "earn" 180 times the wages of their workers and would award themselves multimillion dollar bonuses even in years when

enrollment numbers dropped or professors were laid off. Major components of university curriculum, from introductory composition to intermediate calculus, would be assembled in Mexican maquiladoras (U.S.-owned factories) by "teachers" working for a few dollars a day. University infrastructure and safety standards would gradually erode, to the point at which a minor dent in a classroom wall would cost $1,200, plus labor, to fix, and entire buildings would burst into flames whenever students accidentally bumped into their rear doors.[46]

All kidding aside, the current doctrine of market competition and utilitarian schooling drains education of its most important functions. Aside from delivering skills to students and new products for industry, the primary function of education—and to an unrecognized extent college education—is its socializing effect in introducing students to practices of humanistic inquiry and the sharing of ideas. Some call it the great liberal arts tradition of lifelong learning, in which young people learn, not simply how to wire a circuit or market a TV, but how to continually expand their corpus of knowledge by questioning the world and testing its accepted premises. Slowly some corporations are recognizing the importance of "critical thinking," that is, employees who can find less-than-obvious solutions to problems or "see outside the box."

For all of the positive benefits of "high-productivity" lecture classes and distance learning, educational researchers still tell us that the most efficient learning still takes place among smaller cohorts of students who can interact with their teachers and peers in informal discussion. Even more effective is the sort of one-on-one tutoring and mentorship that result from personal consultations or office visits. All of this highly "inefficient" teaching goes against the grain of a business model of educational management, because it is also difficult to meter, evaluate, or even document in many instances. Yet it is necessary.

Notes

1. Russell Mokhiber and Robert Weissman, "Focus on the Corporation," *Multinational Monitor* (6 November 1998), 2.

2. Lynne V. Cheney, *American Memory: A Report on the Humanities in the Nation's Public Schools* (Washington D.C.: U.S. Government Printing Office, 1987), 5.

3. Samuel Lipman, "Redefining Culture and Democracy," *New Criterion* 8 (December 1989): 16.

4. Peggy Charren, quoted in Holley Knaus, "The Education Industry: The Corporate Takeover of Public Schools," *Corporate Watch*, www.corpwatch.org (6 November 1999).

5. Steven Manning, "Students for Sale: How Corporations Are Buying Their Way into America's Schools," *The Nation* 269, no. 9 (27 September 1999): 11.

6. Susan Herzon, "Selling Out Kids," *Our Children*, www.unm.edu, November 1997 [accessed 12 November 1999].

7. As cited in Rieff, "Multiculturalism's Silent Partner," *Harper's Magazine* 287, no. 1717 (Aug. 1993), 65. See also Richard Ohman, "On 'PC' and Related Matters," in *PC Wars: Politics and Theory in the Academy,* ed. Jeffrey Williams (New York: Routledge, 1995), 11–21.

8. "Hot Type," *Chronicle of Higher Education* (20 July 1994), A10. The statistics were drawn from Steven Brint, *In an Age of Experts: The Changing Role of Professionals in Politics and Political Life* (Princeton, N.J.: Princeton University Press, 1994).

9. Joel Bleifuss, "Building Plans," *In These Times* 19, no. 17 (10 July 1995), 12–15. See also Randy Shaw, *The Activist's Handbook: A Primer for the 1990s and Beyond* (Berkeley: University of California, 1996).

10. William J. Bennett, *To Reclaim a Legacy: A Report on the Humanities in Higher Education* (Washington, D.C.: U.S. Government Printing Office, 1984); T. E. Bell, *A Nation at Risk: The Imperative for Educational Reform* (Washington, D.C.: U.S. Government Printing Office, 1983).

11. E. D. Hirsch Jr., *Cultural Literacy: What Every American Needs to Know* (New York: Vintage, 1987), 20.

12. Paul Lauter, " 'Political Correctness' and the Attack on American Colleges," *Radical Teacher* 44 (Winter 1993): 34–40.

13. Issued in the final year of his presidency, Bush's "America 2000: A Plan for the Nation's Schools" proposed vouchers and a school-choice option, which would allow parents to move their children into private schools at government expense.

14. Svi Shapiro, "Clinton and Education: Policies without Meaning," *Tikkun* 9, no. 3 (May–June 1994): 17–20, 90. An incisive review of Clinton administration education policy appears in a special "Goals 2000" issue of *Teachers College Record* 96, no. 3 (Spring 1995).

15. L. Fraser, "Tyranny of the Media Correct: The Assault on the New McCarthyism," *Extra!* 4, no. 4 (1991): 6.

16. See Jerry Adler, "Taking Offense," *Newsweek,* 24 December 1990, 54.

17. Roger Kimball, *Tenured Radicals: How Politics Has Corrupted Our Higher Education* (New York: Harper and Row, 1990); Dinesh D'Sousa, *Illiberal Education: The Politics of Race and Sex on Campus* (New York: The Free Press, 1991).

18. Kimball, *Tenured Radicals,* 166.

19. D'Sousa, *Illiberal Education,* 257.

20. Adler, "Taking Offense," 54.

21. Rosa Ehrenreich, "What Campus Radicals? The P.C. Undergrad Is a Useful Spectre," in *Are You Politically Correct?: Debating America's Cultural Standards,* ed. F. Beckwith and M. Bauman (New York: Prometheus Books, 1993), 33–39.

22. Gregory S. Jay, "Knowledge, Power, and the Struggle for Representation," *College English* 56, no. 1 (January 1994): 20.

23. Page Smith, *Killing the Spirit: Higher Education in America* (New York: Viking, 1990).

24. Charles J. Sykes, *Profscam: Professors and the Demise of Higher Education* (New York: St. Martin's Press, 1988).

25. Jay, "Knowledge, Power, and the Struggle for Representation," 20.

26. Leon Wieseltier, "All or Nothing at All: The Unreal World of Cornel West," *New Republic*, 6 March 1995, 31.

27. Salim Mukakkil, "The Public Mind," *In These Times* 19, no. 13 (15 May 1995), 25.

28. Brother Patrick Ellis, "The Managerial Presidency According to the AGB," *Change* 30, no. 3 (May/June 1998), 44.

29. Katherine Magnan, "Corporate Know-How Lands Presidencies for a Growing Number of Business Deans," *Chronicle of Higher Education* (27 March 1998), A43–46.

30. Cary Nelson, in *Will Teach for Food: Academic Labor in Crisis*, ed. Cary Nelson (Minneapolis: University of Minnesota Press, 1997), 3–4.

31. Michael Walzer, "The Underworked American," *New Republic*, 22 September 1977.

32. Kevin Robbins and Frank Webster, *Times of the Technoculture: From the Information Society to the Virtual Life* (London and New York: Routledge, 1999), 212. See also Ken Goldberg, ed., *The Robot in the Garden: Telerobotics and Telepistemology in the Age of the Internet* (Cambridge, Mass.: MIT Press, 2000); Michael Margolis and David Resnick, *Politics as Usual: The Cyberspace "Revolution"* (Thousand Oaks, Calif.: Sage, 2000); Ann Travers, *Writing the Public in Cyberspace: Redefining Inclusion on the Net* (London and New York: Garland Publishing, 2000).

33. George Will, "Disorder in Schools," *Time*, 13 April 1998, 84.

34. Michael O'Donovan Anderson, "Ivory Tower: The Big Lie," *Salon*, 25 January 1999, 2.

35. Anderson, "Ivory Tower," 2.

36. Anderson, "Ivory Tower," 2.

37. Anderson, "Ivory Tower," 2.

38. Mike Males, *Scapegoat Generation: America's War on Adolescents* (Monroe, Maine: Common Courage Press, 1996).

39. Andrew Ross, "Introduction," in *Microphone Fiends: Youth Music & Youth Culture*, ed. Andrew Ross and Tricia Rose (New York: Routledge, 1994), 4.

40. Gary Wolfram, "The Threat to Independent Education: Public Subsidies and Private Education," *Cato Policy Analysis* 278 (15 August 1997): 1.

41. Paul Lauter, "Political Correctness," in *Higher Education Under Fire: Politics, Economics, and the Crisis of the Humanities*, ed. Michael Bérubé (New York: Routledge, 1995), 81.

42. Stanley Aronowitz, "Academic Unionism and the Future of Higher Education," in *Will Teach for Food: Academic Labor in Crisis*, ed. Cary Nelson (Minneapolis: University of Minnesota Press, 1997), 188.

43. Aronowitz, "Academic Unionism," 189.

44. Ken Silverstein, "Millions for Viagra: Pennies for the Diseases of the Poor," *The Nation* 269, no. 3 (19 July 1999): 13.

45. James Luh, "Ivory Tower: 'Pact with the CEO,'" *Salon*, 8 February 1999.

46. Michael Bérubé, "Why Inefficiency Is Good for Universities," *Chronicle of Higher Education* (27 March 1998), B5.

4

Welcome to Cyberschool

N o one can deny that education is experiencing one of its most tumultuous periods ever. As schools and universities brace for the approaching tidal wave of baby boomers' children, tensions are worsening over school funding, educational standards, admissions policies, and vouchers—not to mention such hysterically publicized topics as teen sexuality, gang membership, and school violence. The proposed solutions are as varied as the problems themselves, with calls for heightened efficiency in school management, tougher tests and course requirements, increased competition among schools, heightened security, and, of course, stricter discipline. Increasingly technology is seen as the means of implementing these changes.

The single most dramatic factor driving the rush to technology in education is the anticipated growth of the student population. This *echo boom* of offspring of the post–World War II baby boomers hit the secondary school level in the late 1990s. The effect in California alone is a projected need of an additional 260,000 K–12 teachers in the next decade. During that period the number of college-age young people is expected to grow by 20 percent, and the overall enrollments are projected to expand by 40 percent. This profound growth in the student population is occurring at a time when the original cohort of postwar college professors, hired to meet the demands of the baby-boom generation during the 1960s and 1970s, is reaching retirement age. Finally, this decline in the established postsecondary workforce is taking place as the facilities—the classrooms, laboratories, and campus infrastructure—of many colleges and universities built or expanded in the 1960s and 1970s are in need of repair or replacement. In some areas this is even necessitating the construction of new schools.

In the face of this apparent demand for professors and buildings, one might imagine that educational administrators would be planning new hiring initiatives and capital campaigns. Not so. Regrettably, the residue of the back-to-basics reform movements of the 1980s, as well as negative public opinion generated by conservatives toward university-based affirmative action, multiculturalism, "political correctness," and "tenured radicalism," created an atmosphere in which increases in educational funding became all but politically unthinkable, except for kindergarten and elementary school children. Coupled with the corporatization of education discussed in the last chapter, the resource crunch of the 2000s has resulted in calls for greater efficiency in education rather than more school spending.

Rather than replacing retiring tenured professors, the number of temporary, part-time instructors has continued to grow, and increasing responsibilities have been heaped on graduate teaching assistants. Rather than constructing new classrooms, plans have been developed to expand the usage of existing facilities. The most extreme consequence of this has occurred at the community college level, where in some districts classes are being offered twenty-four hours per day, every day of the year. Labor issues aside, this has created a highly compromised—but clearly more cost-efficient—environment for teaching and learning. Propelling this move to efficiency is a new breed of academic administrators, entering the university from the business sector or rising within the university due to their business expertise. As a result, those in decision-making positions within higher education are increasingly sympathetic to critiques of the university as fiscally bloated and unresponsive to "customer" demand. These new administrators are more likely to find solutions to problems based more on utility than pedagogical effectiveness or humanistic concern. At the center of this corporatist reform lies the mechanization of instruction. New forms of distance learning, teleconferencing, computer-mediated instruction, Web and CD-ROM-based curricula are being implemented to increase teacher productivity by enabling the instruction of larger groups of students and the elimination of the need for duplicate presentations.

Back to the Future

Of course, the idea of mechanized instruction isn't new. In the 1920s and 1930s "audiovisual" materials such as sound recordings, slides, and films were widely used in K–12 schooling with the support of the Division of Visual Instruction of the National Educational Association. The newly emerging field of educational psychology supported these new media in the belief that they improved students' experience of school and enhanced their ability to memorize concepts.[1] Significantly, these early proponents of technologically mediated education saw themselves as progressive reformers, not unlike 1960s advocates of television in the classroom, and the current promoters of computerized learning. In the 1920s the Division of Visual Instruction actively lobbied equipment manufacturers and film production companies to enter the educational market. It also convinced the military of the importance of audiovisual media, both as a means of training troops and as a propaganda tool. Missing in these early formulations was any consideration of problematic ways that filmic media can structure the educational experience as a one-directional, nondialogical, transmission—especially at a time when people were unaccustomed to engaging media critically.

By 1945 the federal government had entered the picture, allocating support for audiovisual education in public schools through the Vocational Education Act. In what Anne De Vaney calls the "stellar modern project" of media education, the merger of mind and machine was touted as an emblem of U.S. industrial, military, and intellectual might. Like today, corporations were the driving force for this mechanization of education in vocational terms—as students were simultaneously constructed as objects to be serviced, consumers to be won, and workers to be trained.

As the first wave of the baby boom hit the classroom in the 1960s, video became recognized as a means of increasing teacher productivity. By simply eliminating the need for duplicate presentations, video was credited with reductions in labor of up to 70 percent.[2] It was also recognized as a powerful tool for observation and evaluation.[3] Concurrent advances in computer and telecommunications industries prompted more elaborate speculation. While in residence at New York's Fordham University during the late 1960s, Marshall McLuhan attracted a quasireligious following based on his vision of a global telecommunications network designed on biological (and therefore "natural") principles that would undermine all hierarchical structures. At the core of McLuhan's program lay a concept of media as "information without content" that defined international turmoil as the result of failed communication rather than ideological confrontation.[4]

This idealistic vision of new technology fit perfectly into 1960s educational reformism, while also complementing U.S. cultural policy. In a domestic atmosphere of desegregation, urban renewal, and other liberal initiatives, efforts were made to eliminate the biases inherent in standard pedagogies. As a means of de-emphasizing differences of race, gender, and class, theories of educational formalism were introduced into many schools to stress the structure of learning over culturally specific content. Educators uncritically seized upon photographic media as tools for directly engaging student experience. They developed concepts of "visual literacy" to compete with what some viewed as oppressive print-oriented paradigms.[5] As one educational textbook of the era explained, many students "demonstrate a lack of proficiency and lack of interest in reading and writing. Can we really expect proficiency when interest is absent? To what purpose do we force students through traditional subjects in traditional curricula?"[6] Within this movement, many teachers adapted photography and video equipment to teach subjects ranging from social studies to English composition.

With the economic downturns of the 1980s and the ascent of the Reagan/ Bush government came sweeping indictments of liberal programs. Supply-side analysts blamed schools for the nation's inability to compete in world markets, while ironically arguing for reductions in federal education and cultural budgets. Because they often required expensive equipment, media programs were terminated in the name of cost reduction, as renewed emphasis was placed on a back-to-basics curriculum. This did not mean that television disappeared from the classroom, only that its more complicated, hands-on, applications were replaced by simple viewing.

The type of media that survived the reform movements of the early 1980s differed greatly from its utopian predecessors. Stripped of any remnant of formalist ideology, video was reduced to its utilitarian function as a labor-saving device. This redefinition of "television as teacher" paralleled distinct shifts in production and distribution. These were outgrowths of large-scale changes in the film and television industry brought about by the emergence of affordable videocassette equipment. For the viewer, home recording and tape rental allowed unprecedented control over what was watched. The same was true in the classroom. For the instructional media industry, the costly process of copying 16mm films was quickly supplanted by inexpensive high-speed video duplication. The entire concept of educational media products began to change, as films could be mass produced on a national scale (in effect, "published") like books. Market expansion in this type of video was exponential. So profound was the technological change that 16mm film-processing labs from coast to coast went out of business practically overnight. The shape of education was changed forever.

Computers didn't become a serious part of K–12 schooling until the 1990s, with the broad-based distribution of personal computers in the home, the development of network technology, and the popular advocacy of computers in education by public figures such as Al Gore and Bill Gates. Like cable television, the Internet was touted as a means of bringing the outside world into the classroom, while connecting students to resources hitherto unimagined. In its early stages of implementation, school computerization was also regarded as a means of leveling the cultural differences among students— much as "visual literacy" had been promoted. These attitudes fit well within the progressive belief that digital media could deliver a world of great equity and freedom. From this perspective, public education should be seen as an extremely important means of redressing technological inequities, and their inherent relationships with race, gender, geography, and social class. Not only can schools serve as places to provide access and instruction to digital media, but they can also structure the experience of these media through progressive pedagogies that critically engage technologies and foster equity and student agency.

Cyberschool Today

Is the current craze for computers in the classroom simply an extension of this historical faith in educational mechanization, or is it something more? The business interests that have the most to gain in this matter assert that fundamental structural changes and paradigm shifts are occurring that necessitate new technological approaches to schooling. This could be dismissed as simple self-interest were it not that high-tech corporations are playing a growing role in educational policy discussions. Meanwhile, parents exposed to an endless barrage of effusive media reports and advertising about the "information society" and the need for "digital literacy" are petrified at the idea of their kids missing out. So it's a double whammy. As parents pressure schools to adopt technology, schools are becoming institutional customers for educational products and venues for promotions targeted at students. It's an entrepreneurial dream come true. Fortunately, there are limits to ways that K–12 schools can change. Given the role of schools as day care for underage youth, the fundamental structure of schools and the school day will not change significantly. Since elementary and secondary schools are also primarily regarded as a site for general academic or vocational education, the fundamental balance in curriculum among humanities, science, and math offerings will similarly resist significant change. This stability is further buttressed by the decentralized governance of schools at the level of the local school district and the high degree of political scrutiny that communities afford to educational issues.

This raises the crucial issue of computer competency, or what has been termed *digital literacy*. Despite the popular notion of young people as naturally computer-savvy, a need exists at the university to instill critical sensibilities toward digital media much like those offered by television- and film-oriented media literacy programs. Partly informed by critical pedagogy and cultural studies, the digital literacy movement (as opposed to its older "market research" counterpart) is an amalgam of reader response theories and institutional analyses. While acknowledging the persuasive properties of images, practitioners of digital literacy emphasize ways that viewers use media in individualized ways. Moreover, because Web surfers and computer-game players can recognize the artifice of representation, they need not always be fooled by it. The concept of literacy is central in this pedagogy; as explained by Cary Bazalgette, "Every medium can be thought of as a language. Every medium has its own way of organizing meaning, and we all learn to 'read' it, bringing our own understandings to it, and extending our own experience through it."[7]

In this sense, the digital literacy movement holds political significance. Not only can it help viewers "decode" complex sign systems, but it also can connect theory and practice—often by attempting to literally explain (or demonstrate) complex theories to young people. By doing this it diplomatically reconciles opposing concepts of the viewing subject. In textual terms, the digital literacy movement argues that our abilities to mediate dominant readings and spectator positioning can be improved with study and that these skills can be taught to children regardless of age or grade level. Young people can use digital tools for their own ends by learning to actively interpret how they function and then choosing how to use them. Put another way, the movement proposes to begin identifying strategies for contextual reading, thereby suggesting changes to the "institutional structures" that condition spoken and interpretive norms.[8] This is done by encouraging viewers to look beyond specific texts by asking critical questions like "Who is communicating and why?" "How is it produced?" "Who receives it and what sense do they make of it?"

But not everyone is happy about digital literacy programs. As the practice of teaching students how to read and critique the medium has grown and been promoted, many educators believe its methods are shallow and that it diverts resources from much-needed basics. While such arguments originally were heard from conservative reformers two decades ago, now they come from progressives as well. Jonathan Sterne states, "The very idea of computer literacy is conflicted at its core: while educators clearly intended computer literacy as the ability to control machines, the language of literacy can easily degenerate into the project of creating consumer populations for communications technologies."[9] While traditional literacy programs are premised on the ability to both read and write, digital literacy tends to focus only on using or viewing software programs, Web sites, and CD-ROMs. The key notion of writing or producing exists only as an intellectual response, rendering digital literacy programs lessons in consumption. As David Bolt and Ray Crawford write in *The Digital Divide*,

> When you put computer literacy before literacy, the only thing you are doing is turning out people who do not have a complete facility with either. The com-

puter, for all of its audio and graphic qualities, is still primarily a written medium, words on a screen. If people cannot create readable, understandable, and relevant content, then having a computer is of little or no value to them.[10]

Other critics of digital literacy education argue that computer technology in general, and especially in educational context, further promotes hierarchies separating technology-rich and -poor students. Suzanne K. Damarin has pointed out how most computer-oriented instruction mitigates against a respect for cultural difference in its overdetermination by scientific objectivism.[11] Simply put, the literature of computing is founded on principles of scientific neutrality and empirical absolutism. Such paradigms reinforce center/margin dichotomies and mitigate against a tolerance of difference. For all of the claims made that computer networks and hypertext writing deconstruct and destabilize the subject "in theory," the practical application of information technology in schools relies on a set of prescriptive norms and functionalist goals. Finally, school economists assert that digital literacy programs are especially damaging for disadvantaged schools, who feel pressured to add computer-oriented courses at the expense of other offerings. As Bolt and Crawford put it, this may be more than a simple zero-sum game. Parents and schools should exercise extreme caution in deciding "whether cutting programs to put in technology which does not have a demonstrated and documented effectiveness in learning and may, in fact, have a negative effect on children's long-term development, is worth the short-term peace of mind brought by blindly believing that this technology is 'the answer.' "[12]

The Cyberdivide in Schools

Much like the digital divide that exists among social groups within the United States, serious technological inequalities persist in the nation's schools. To a great extent these inequalities parallel disparities in school funding between wealthy and impoverished school districts. Yet there are other independent causes relating to technology as well. In many ways the cyberdivide between schools is far more significant than the digital divide among adult users, considering the importance of schooling in determining lifelong patterns of learning and behavior. The digital literacy movement may be propelled by commercial hype and parental anxiety, but the role of computers and the Internet in decades to come is beyond dispute. Hence the cyberdivide in schools and the broader economic injustice that causes this divide demand serious public policy consideration.

In his farewell address to the 2000 Democratic National Convention, Bill

Clinton proudly stated that 95 percent of the nation's public schools had been connected to the Internet. Clinton failed to mention how many schools had *only* an Internet connection—and little else in terms of network or computer capacity. The reality is that the majority of the nation's schools do not have directly allocated funds for telecommunication, nor do they possess the infrastructure to support computers they might receive from industry or government. Getting connected is important. But so is having an internal network and workstations, which regularly need service and replacement. Donations or equipment grants of computers can be wonderful for schools—until the need is recognized for ongoing technology budgets and technical support personnel. Most schools still lack this broader complement of resources. Of those that do not, many have faculty that are unprepared to use computers in the classroom. At one third of the nation's schools, three quarters of the teachers do not own a home computer.[13] Indeed, studies show that less than 20 percent of schools consider themselves "well prepared" to deliver technology education.[14]

As the problem of the digital divide for individuals became an issue in the mainstream politics and media in 1999 and 2000, the corporate sector asserted that falling computer prices and the proliferation of no-cost Internet services would soon solve the problem. To some extent this did indeed help, especially as the computer and software industries came to recognize underserved groups and communities of color as untapped "niche" markets. But this did little to obviate the school dilemma. In reviewing the history of the school divide, Sterne begins with a simple hypothesis: If White people had an advantage over people of color in learning computing and access to computers, it would help explain the current Whiteness of the Internet.[15] Indeed this was the case. From the beginning, well-financed schools in predominantly White suburbs and affluent areas were more likely to have Internet connections, fiber-optic systems, phone jacks in classrooms, and other necessities of cyberspace. They also were more likely, at least in the 1980s, to be among the first recipients of donations by computer companies. Before the personal computer revolution became a reality, hardware companies—most notably Apple—regarded schools as ideal opportunities for product placement to develop customer bases. When companies did make donations to poor schools, it was often in the service of public relations. As Sterne writes,

> Clearly, Apple's philanthropic goals were complementary to its commercial goals. It favored educators who were already plugged into larger professional networks (i.e., "jointly planned"), and who already had some access to computing resources and some basic computer knowledge. As a result, these philanthropic goals helped perpetuate existing stratification of access to computers.[16]

Owing to the interest in the digital divide from the federal government and private groups like the Benton and Markle Foundations, significant public attention has been focused on the issue of wiring and equipping the nation's schools. The biggest danger now is that wiring the schools may become, in the public mind, a substitute for actual school financing reform. As the Markle Foundation's Andrew Blau states, "Computers are not a silver bullet for what may be ailing public education today."[17] By focusing too much attention on the computer issue, we may not only be ignoring root causes of school inequality, we may well be making them worse.

Cybercollege

College is another story altogether—one in which mechanization and corporate influences are transforming institutional organization, governance, curriculum, and research in profound ways. In a report titled "The Virtual University," great changes during the next decade were predicted by senior administrators and business people from a diverse range of institutions that included IBM, Lotus, Educom, National Science Foundation, Pew Charitable Trusts, Sloan Foundation, and American Federation of Teachers, as well as the universities of California, Hawaii, Illinois, Michigan, Minnesota, and Virginia.[18] The document anticipates a restructuring of postsecondary education in the first decade of the twenty-first century, as conventional residential four-year colleges and universities change or go out of business. These will be replaced by "a global electronic campus, which students enter via a computer and thereby telecommute from home, a dormitory room, the workplace, or a community center," and "the continuing education and training provided by employers and community organizations."[19]

Echoing many of the familiar refrains about a rapidly changing technological work world, the report projects the need for employees to retrain for "six to seven different careers in the course of a lifetime" and that within five years 75 percent of all workers will need retraining. Computer skills, currently used by 65 percent of workers, will be used by 95 percent of employees in the first years of the new millennium. Citing a survey by the National Home Business Association, the report asserts that the number of people working from a home office will rise from 29 million to 50 percent of the working population. Exacerbating the need for technology even further is the exponentially growing volume of information that workers will need to be able to use, with the corpus of all human knowledge doubling every seven years.

These changes in the world of business, work, and information will generate new demands from students. As Educom/IBM puts it, "Students expect to participate in a learning environment that fosters measurable improvement in their skill development, not just during college, but also throughout their careers. Students are increasingly selecting curricula that enhance their chances of both initial and sustained employment."[20] This pressure will force traditional colleges and universities to change their offerings and modes of curricular delivery as they seek "a competitive edge in a student based—or consumer driven—market."[21] Finally, since it will be difficult for bureaucracy-laden universities to change quickly, much of this new education will be delivered by private enterprises like ITT Technical, Heald Institute, and the University of Phoenix. In summary, in the next decade higher education will take on the following attributes:

> Institutions develop and maintain programs through a continuous process of market research. . . . External feedback is an integral part of all programs. Most students are not seeking degrees. Instead modularization enables them to meet their particular learning needs, often tied to job or career goals. The faculty role has changed. As a greater amount of codified knowledge is captured in courseware, the role of the faculty member is increasingly that of a mentor or leader in the learning process. Faculty labor is applied at times and in circumstances when it is needed—that is, on-demand—rather than on a fixed schedule.[22]

The brave new world of education predicted in the Educom/IBM report is already upon us. The Western Governors University (WGU), a "virtual campus" established by the governors of fifteen states, is a publicly funded, market-oriented, degree-granting entity organized on precisely the principles of competition and "customer-driven" content described previously. It incorporates the services of numerous third-party providers like ATT, IBM, Cisco Systems, and Novell to provide, not only equipment and software, but also instructional materials and curricular content. The WGU is expressly intended to compete with private sector providers of just-in-time, modularized instruction. The university has no faculty of its own, but relies instead on affiliated institutions and databases for course delivery. Planners predict that by 2005 the WGU will generate $125 million per year in revenues.[23]

Meanwhile, private, for-profit versions of the virtual university are popping up everywhere, the most ubiquitous of which is the University of Phoenix. With fifty thousand students it is already the largest private university in the country. However, it has not accomplished this success by establishing anything resembling a campus. Many University of Phoenix students take their courses online or at drop-in locations at any of its ninety satellite locations, mostly located in rented office space. Catering to the growing adult population of people anxious about their job skills (euphemistically termed *lifelong learners*), the University of Phoenix has no tenured faculty.[24]

But at least the University of Phoenix operates within the law. In an era in which a college degree is seen as a prerequisite to many well-paying jobs, the much-publicized distance-learning craze has a criminal dark side in the rapid growth of fraudulent Internet "diploma mills." Columbia State University on the World Wide Web, for example, has been aggressively promoting itself in newspapers around the country as a place where one can get a bachelor's degree in twenty-seven days. The Higher Education Research Institute in Hawaii offers a bachelor's degree in journalism in exchange for $1,800 and a two-thousand-word thesis. These unregulated and unaccredited institutions capitalize on the desperation of people who fall prey to the belief that technology can somehow deliver the education or at least the credentials that other more conventional means cannot. Although advocates of legitimate distance learning are quick to point out that even an unaccredited institution can—in principle—deliver high-quality instruction, this is regrettably not the case in a growing number of online institutions. As journalist Lisa Guernsey wrote in the *Chronicle of Higher Education,*

> Colleges that provide low-quality education—or none at all—and at the same time pass themselves off as leaders in distance education are dangerous. . . . Not only do they cheapen the value of degrees and trick unwitting employers into hiring people who may not have the skills they profess to have, but they can taint all distance-education programs as something to avoid.[25]

But these are only the most obvious examples of a much broader phenomenon taking place inside almost all colleges and universities, as campus after campus begins to slowly expand vocational/technical curricula and reduce academic/humanistic offerings. This reapportioning of instructional content is accompanied by incentives—or in some cases requirements to technologize teaching. In the most benign instances, this might mean simply posting a syllabus on the Internet or being available to students via e-mail. Elsewhere, faculty are encouraged to translate course materials into video formats or software programs that can be accessed on demand or from remote locations.

These practices present potential problems in the way they fragment or extend academic labor, remove instructors from the pedagogical process, and permit growing levels of administrative monitoring, control, and intervention in the way education takes place. In a widely reproduced essay titled "Digital Diploma Mills," David Noble discusses the worrisome implications of the new virtual university. He writes,

> What is driving this headlong rush to implement new technology with so little regard for the pedagogical and economic costs, and at the risk of student and

faculty alienation? A short answer might be the fear of getting left behind, the incessant pressures of "progress." But there is more to it. For universities are not simply undergoing technological transformation. Beneath that change, and camouflaged by it, lies another: the commercialization of higher education. For here as elsewhere technology is but a vehicle and a disarming disguise.[26]

According to Noble, universities are undergoing a change that has been occurring for the last two decades, as the university is transformed from a relatively autonomous nonprofit educational provider into a significant site of corporately regulated capital accumulation. In a two-stage process that began with the commodification of research, the university has become increasingly reliant upon and influenced by the mandates of commercial product development. This began in the wake of the 1970s oil crisis and the concomitant decline in heavy industry, as business and political leaders began to recognize the potential in value-added goods, service industries, and "knowledge-based" products. The latter recognition of "intellectual capital" as a potentially lucrative form of currency both enabled and benefited from the information technology boom of the last decade. The ubiquity of home computers and network access among the privileged classes of the world's wealthier nations, as well as the growing role of these technologies in research of all kinds, made it possible for universities to become the new labs and manufacturing plants for saleable knowledge.

In more recent years, the second stage of this transformation has emerged, in which the educational function of the university is similarly co-opted and commodified, both in the way curricula are organized and delivered, and in the development and sale of copyrighted videos, courseware, CD-ROMs, and Web services. In the process professors become the unwitting or unwilling agents of an educational enterprise far different from the one they entered. As Noble writes, "To some what began in the 1970s as a bottom-line approach to research has changed in the 1990s to an approach to instruction that stresses productivity and efficiency over pedagogical concern."[27] Noble continues,

> Major promoters of this transformation are university administrators, who see it as a way of giving their institutions a fashionable forward-looking image. More importantly, they view computer-based instruction as a means of reducing their direct labor and plant maintenance costs—fewer teachers and classrooms—while at the same time undermining the autonomy and independence of faculty.[28]

Ultimately, this digitization of higher education represents much more than a labor issue. More than one commentator has suggested, following the Educom/IBM reasoning, that computer networks will eliminate the need for costly campuses, troublesome faculty, and the numerous other inconveniences that define college. David Cohen writes that "this technology would eliminate the need for universities to provide day care for superannuated adolescents: The costly and burdensome administration of dormitories, health services, counseling, and related services could be reduced or eliminated."[29]

But even those campuses immune from the threat of being rendered redundant or obsolete by new technology are changing in worrisome ways. Students at wealthy private colleges and research universities have been exposed to new learning technologies for some time. But they are now experiencing something new, as computer security and identification systems accompany them throughout the campus. The ubiquitous student ID card is now commonly encoded with an electromagnetic strip that allows it to function as library card or cafeteria meal ticket. However, at Princeton University, Yale, and a number of other institutions, so-called proximity cards—or prox cards—are also being used as keys to allow student access to dorms, labs, and other facilities. Digital technology allows such cards to be individually tailored to allow individuals access to dozens of different doors at different times of the day. At the same time, they enable the university to record an individual's movement through the campus—something the university indeed does. After the card system was implemented at Princeton, 80 percent of men and 60 percent of women students polled said they didn't want the kind of twenty-four-hour invasion of privacy the prox cards created. Yet the Princeton administration retained the system.[30]

These many changes within higher education are producing a highly charged and polarized discourse. Discussing the introduction of information technology into the academic classroom, Martin Trow has identified three general motives: (1) the enrichment of instruction, (2) expanded access to education, and (3) cost containment.[31] Trow makes the important point that introduction of technology in the classroom is an inevitability. What remains to be determined is exactly how that introduction will take place. Certainly university administrators do not constitute a monolith, even if their ranks are increasingly filled by business people. At this early stage in the game, considerable flexibility still exists for progressive means of structuring the technologization of higher education. Faculty have an important role to play, as they always have had, in directing the course of this work.

Technology will not enter all colleges in the same way or for the same purposes. By far the most advanced kinds of computer "courseware" are currently developed and used for basic or remedial instruction, especially in language skills. Such materials are used most in community colleges, which operate with the mission of imparting basic skills to large numbers of students. Less dependent on students seeking complete four-year degrees, community colleges also generate the majority of distance-learning offerings. University extension programs are the second-largest users of computer-based instruction, with research universities and liberal arts colleges entering the computerized instruction game last. Here the university administration plays an important role, not only in encouraging mechanization to take place, but in providing the infrastructure and support personnel to facilitate the process. Indeed, it is all too common to find institutions that are equipment rich but that lack the essential staff to assist in instructional design, implementation, service, and teaching assistance.

It's also important to recognize differences in the kinds of computerized instructional materials that are used. While large corporate courseware developers produce prepackaged instructional modules complete with content and assessment components, energetic faculty at many schools are developing their own courseware tailored to particular subject matter and pedagogical methodology. As in noncomputerized instruction, where it is easier to order a textbook from the bookstore than to assemble or to write one, the ability of faculty to engage in courseware production hinges on a confluence of personal desire and institutional support.

Many factors frustrate this development of courseware. In addition to the enormous amount of time and the requisite technical support that faculty need to produce new courseware lies a more fundamental problem in the university's attitude toward such work.[32] Promotion and tenure committees at most colleges and universities still privilege "research" as the most valuable category of academic work, an attitude supported even more strongly in the current bottom-line atmosphere of higher education administration. The development of courseware is seen as either a "teaching" effort, like that of writing a textbook, or a form of university or public service. Carolyn C. Lougee has identified other factors that are impairing the ability of faculty to continue the courseware development conversation:

> Why has change been so slow? Numerous answers have been proffered: the nature of computerization, "the natural inertia of the university," the high cost of state-of-the-art technology in an age of shrinking budgets. The inability to demonstrate the actual benefits (financial as well as educational), competitive mystifications, and resistance from faculty. . . . [and] Heideggerian fear that technology is dehumanizing, or the anti-practical element in humanists' self-image that make them proudly proclaim "the luxury of incompetence."[33]

As a consequence, faculty are whipsawed over the impulse to computerize—urged by administrators to get up-to-date but uncompensated by peer faculty committees if they take time away from traditional research.

Utopia Revisited

Faculty and students who find themselves in a changing technological environment face the choice of engaging or resisting that change. The discourse of technology is fond of predicting the future with an air of certainty, suggesting that no alternative paths are possible. Yet the history of antitrust suits brought against the radio and telephone industries, the community-based campaigns that have imposed regulations on the cable companies, and more recent efforts for democratic Internet policy have shown that the business world's version of technological utopia is not always the one that prevails. As Michel Foucault has written, power is hardly an absolute force that flows uniformly in one direction.[34] Instead it is a malleable substance with many currents and an eternal possibility of reversal for change. Just as new relationships with entities outside the university constitute cause for worry and concern, they also can be seen as opportunities for positive growth and innovation. The challenge is to engage the possibilities that these new technologies offer, while being cautious of how they may silently undermine the institution. This position is well articulated by William Mitchell in his book *e-topia:*

> The increasingly boring digiphiles and digiphobes, with their contending visions of utopia and dystopia, are myopically groping different extremes of the pachyderm. We will do far better to sidestep the well-known trap of technological determinism, to renounce the symmetrical form of fatalism proposed by booster-technocrats and curmudgeonly techno-scoffers, and begin, instead, by developing a broad, critical, action-oriented perspective on the technological, economic, social, and cultural reality of what's actually going on, all around us, right now. Our job is to design the future we want, not to predict its predetermined path.[35]

The most obvious changes enabled by information technology within universities are structural, with many institutions adapting buildings to new purposes, equipping new labs, identifying new degrees or curricular emphases—to facilitate computer-oriented instruction and research. The use of computer databases and multimedia instruction is transforming the design of libraries and classrooms. And regardless of one's feelings about the Internet, networked communication is altering the way students and faculty study, teach, research, and socialize inside and outside the university. The Net also is enabling scholarship that once took place in the isolation of discrete campuses to become networked into a matrix of knowledge.

This has obvious implications for instruction. To begin with, interdisciplinarity, which for decades was resisted by traditional scholars with interests in preserving protected domains of knowledge and the intellectual hierarchies they held in place, is now so integral to the digital experience that it seems natural. From hyperlinked texts that enable the immediate referencing of ideas throughout the library to Web pages that combine information in written, pictorial, and aural form, notions of linguistic singularity or objective decontextualization seem increasingly remote. At the same time, it is important to note that the curricular interdisciplinarity evoked by digital media also is increasingly celebrated by cost-cutting administrators as a means of reducing instructional labor through compression. Now language programs are compressed into schools of "communication" as multiple art and design specializations are merged into "digital imaging" programs. Hence with each new interdisciplinary program or major that is developed, a countervailing concern needs to be raised for what may be lost in a zero-sum game.

The digitization of instruction offers important opportunities to bring new volumes of material to students and to connect learning in multimedia dimensionality to worlds outside the classroom. Networked bulletin boards, chat rooms, and Web-based virtual spaces offer the ability to bring students together to exchange ideas and collaborate in ways that only the most skilled pedagogue might engineer in a physical classroom. At the same time, instruction mediated by a computer can also engender distraction, laziness, and alienation if students become disengaged in a multimedia classroom or if they lose motivation in the solitary confines of a remote home computer. Indeed, one of the little publicized actualities of the much-touted revolution in distance learning is that the majority of students who begin such courses never finish them. Hardly the future of instruction for all students, professionals who conduct distance-learning courses report that such formats work primarily for students with a supervening reason to use the network, such as students with physical disabilities, residents of rural communities, or homebound child-care providers.

The Store of Knowledge

Increasingly higher education is regarded as the prime site of knowledge production in the information economy, as corporations build partnerships and licensing agreements with colleges and universities around the world. Partly a function of the university's growing willingness to conduct paid commercial research, these relationships also are driven by the changing character of commodities themselves. In a world in which images and concepts are assuming more economic significance than conventional goods and services, centers of idea production become centers of income production. Jeremy Rifkin states that "tangible property is becoming increasingly marginal to the exercise of economic power, and intangible property is fast becoming the defining force in an access-based era."[36] He adds that "ideas in the form of patents, copyrights, trademarks, trade secrets, and relationships—are being used to forge a new kind of economic power composed of megasuppliers in control of expanded networks of users."[37]

On one level this produces numerous new funding opportunities for research efforts in the form of grants, capital contributions, endowed professorships, building campaigns, and even the development of new schools and colleges. Unfortunately this is hardly an equitable form of development, as science and engineering programs, and other computer-related disciplines, enjoy the lion's share of these benefits. But the unevenness extends beyond direct sponsorships, as Richard L. Venezky explains:

> This inequality might be accepted as an inevitable aberration, well-confined and benign, except that the migration of faculty to high-technology centers and the deeper involvement of remaining faculty with industry (sometimes to the point of divided appointments) further reduces the ability of colleges and universities to be intellectual institutions, immune from the pressures and constraints of business and politics.[38]

Even more significant, disciplines in the humanities and social sciences, as well as the noncomputer-based arts, fall victim to an incremental decline, as new, more lucrative, research opportunities pass them by in favor of more directly profitable areas.

To the corporate sector the solution to this dilemma of exclusion is adaptability: the university simply needs to learn how to change along with the times. Setting aside for a moment the impulse to ask why profit-hungry businesses should be telling the university what to do, the fact remains that the growing bifurcation of university departments into haves and have-nots does relate to the way knowledge itself is changing. Back-to-basics Ludditism notwithstanding, academic disciplines of all kinds continue to expand and fragment at a rapid pace, with more than a thousand different undergraduate and graduate majors and programs offered at colleges and universities in the United States. By their very structure, computer networks allow more discrete research collaborations and intellectual communities to develop to further this specialization. To writers such as Neil Postman and John Naisbett, the information explosion produced a deleterious effect in producing a world that is "wallowing in detail, drowning in information, but is starved for knowledge."[39] To others, there exists tremendous opportunity in the ability to access exponentially larger amounts of information than in the past. Always the advocate of a hypertext universe, Richard Lanham asserts that digital media have created a new intellectual "operating system" to replace thinking premised on the structure of the book. Lanham writes,

> It changes the central humanistic artifact (the CPU, we might call it) from printed to digital display. It changes what we mean by author. It undermines the basic idea of originality we inherited from the Romantic Movement. It changes what we mean by text. It radically compromises the cultural authority of the text. It metamorphoses the marketplace of humanistic inquiry in ways so radical we can scarcely find our way. It desubstantiates the arts and letters in much the same way the information society has desubstantiated the industrial revolution.[40]

Among other things, information technology dramatically increases the speed of knowledge sharing and development. Scholarship that once took months or years to get into print can now be electronically "published" immediately. Responses can take a matter of minutes. The effect of this is to destabilize the temporality of knowledge, to undermine its concreteness, and to mitigate against its ownership. This is occurring at a time when libraries and museums are recognizing the new roles they can play as information brokers. The federal government's Digital Library Initiative is dispensing more than $50 million to assist universities in developing new ways to collect, organize, and disseminate data for domestic and military purposes, with partners that include the National Science Foundation, the Library of Congress, NASA, the Department of Defense, as well as universities including Stanford, Carnegie Melon, and those of Illinois, California, and others.

Tempting as it is to assert that information technology is transforming educational institutions at all levels, it is important to recognize that these are not autonomous transformations. Information technology is simply an enabler for deeper social technologies. Much of this chapter has dealt with the way digital media are facilitating the growing privatization of the university and its transformation into an educational marketplace. Schools become sites for commerce, students turn into commodities, and research shifts to product development. Yet at the same time, great potential exists in the way information technology is causing schools and universities to scrutinize themselves and focus more on issues such as the relationship between teaching and research. Ultimately, technology can serve as an important catalyst for the reconceptualization of educational institutions, if it can be seen in such a way.

Notes

1. See Anne De Vaney, "Can and Need Educational Technology Become a Postmodern Enterprise?" *Theory and Practice* 37, no. 1 (Winter 1998): 72–80.

2. Robert M. Diamond, "Single Room Television," in *A Guide to Instructional Media,* ed. Robert M. Diamond (New York: McGraw-Hill, 1964), 3.

3. John M. Hofstrand, "Television and Classroom Observation," in *A Guide to Instructional Media,* ed. Robert M. Diamond (New York: McGraw-Hill, 1964), 149.

4. Marshall McLuhan, *Understanding Media: Extensions of Man* (New York: McGraw-Hill, 1964), 23.

5. The terms *visual literacy* and *media literacy* have been employed in a variety of contexts during the past two decades. The formalist media literacy of the 1970s should not be confused with the critical media literacy movement of the 1980s and 1990s.

6. Linda R. Burnett and Frederick Goldman, *Need Johnny Read? Practical Methods to Enrich Humanities Courses Using Films and Film Studies* (Dayton, Ohio: Pflaum, 1971), xv.

7. Cary Bazalgette, as quoted in Ben Moore, "Media Education," in *The Media Studies Book,* ed. David Lusted (London and New York: Routledge, 1991), 172.

8. Stanley Fish, *Is There a Text in This Class? The Authority of Interpretive Communities* (Cambridge: Harvard University Press, 1980).

9. Jonathan Sterne, "The Computer Race Goes to School," in *Race in Cyberspace,* ed. Beth Kolko et al. (New York and London: Routledge, 2000), 192.

10. David Bolt and Ray Crawford, *The Digital Divide: Computers and Our Children's Future* (New York: TV Books, 2000), 114.

11. Suzanne K. Damarin, "Technology and Multicultural Education: The Question of Convergence," *Theory into Practice* 37, no. 1 (Winter 1998): 11–19.

12. Bolt and Crawford, *The Digital Divide,* 44.

13. Bolt and Crawford, *The Digital Divide,* 35.

14. Bolt and Crawford, *The Digital Divide,* 26.

15. Sterne, "The Computer Race Goes to School," 191.

16. Sterne, "The Computer Race Goes to School," 206.

17. Bolt and Crawford, *The Digital Divide,* 32.

18. Carol Twigg and Diana Oblinger, "The Virtual University" (report from a Joint Educom/IBM Roundtable, Washington, D.C., 5–6 November 1996).

19. Twigg and Oblinger, "The Virtual University," 1.

20. Twigg and Oblinger, "The Virtual University," 5.

21. Twigg and Oblinger, "The Virtual University," 6.

22. Twigg and Oblinger, "The Virtual University," 9–10.

23. Goldie Blumenstyk, "Western Governors U. Takes Shape as a New Model for Higher Education," *Chronicle of Higher Education* XLIV, no. 17 (6 February 1998): A21.

24. Michael Margolis, "Brave New Universities," *First Monday,* http://www.firstmonday.dk/issues/issue3_5/margolis/, 1998 [accessed 10 November 1999].

25. Lisa Guernsey, "Is the Internet Becoming a Bonanza for Diploma Mills?" *Chronicle of Higher Education* XLIII, no. 7 (19 December 1997): A22.

26. David F. Noble, "Digital Diploma Mills," *First Monday,* www.firstmonday.dk/issues/issue3_1/noble, 5 January 1998 [accessed 10 October 1999].

27. Noble, "Digital Diploma Mills."

28. Noble, "Digital Diploma Mills."

29. David Cohen, "Educational Technology and School Organization," in *Technology in Education: Looking Forward Toward 2020*, ed. Raymond S. Nickerson and Philip P. Zodhiates (Hillsdale, N.J.: Erlbaum, 1988), 238–239.

30. Peter Wayner, "Closed Door Policy," *New York Times*, 12 November 1998, D1, 8.

31. Martin Trow, "The Development of Information Technology in Higher Education," *Daedalus* 126, no. 4 (Fall 1997): 293–314.

32. Richard A. Lanham, "The Implications of Electronic Information for the Sociology of Knowledge," *Leonardo* 27, no. 2 (1994): 156. See also David Bell and Barbara Kennedy, eds., *The Cybercultures Reader* (London and New York: Routledge, 2000); Stephanie Gibson and Ollie Oviedo, eds., *The Emerging Cyberculture: Literacy, Paradigm, and Paradox* (Cresskill, N.J.: Hampton Press, 2000); Ann Travers, *Writing the Public in Cyberspace: Redefining Inclusion on the Net* (London and New York: Garland Publishing, 2000).

33. Carolyn C. Lougee, "The Professional Implications of Electronic Information," *Leonardo* 27, no. 2 (1994): 148.

34. Michel Foucault, *Discipline and Punish: The Birth of the Prison*, trans. Alan Sheridan (New York: Vintage, 1975), 225.

35. William J. Mitchell, *e-topia: "Urban Life, Jim—But Not as We Know It"* (Cambridge, Mass.: MIT Press, 1999), 12.

36. Jeremy Rifkin, *The Age of Access: The New Culture of Hypercapitalism, Where All of Life Is a Paid-for Experience* (New York: Putnam, 2000), 57.

37. Rifkin, *The Age of Access*, 57.

38. Richard L. Venezky, "The Impact of Computer Technology on Higher Education, in *The American University: Problems, Prospects, Trends*, ed. Jan H. Blits (Buffalo: SUNY, 1985), 63.

39. Neil Postman, *Technopoly: The Surrender of Culture to Technology* (New York: Vintage Books, 1993), 69. See also John Naisbett, *Megatrends: Ten New Directions for the 1990s* (New York: Avon Books, 1990); Ken Goldberg, ed., *The Robot in the Garden: Telerobotics and Telepistemology in the Age of the Internet* (Cambridge, Mass.: MIT Press, 2000); Gill Kirkup et al., eds., *The Gendered Cyborg: A Reader* (London and New York: Routledge, 2000); Peter Lunenfeld, *Snap to Grid: A Users Guide to Digital Arts, Media, and Cultures* (Cambridge, Mass.: MIT Press, 2000); Michael Margolis and David Resnick, *Politics as Usual: The Cyberspace "Revolution"* (Thousand Oaks, Calif.: Sage, 2000).

40. Lanham, "The Implications of Electronic Information," 156.

5

Myths of Cyberdemocracy

WE LIVE IN AN ERA of democratic contradiction. As the Cold War recedes into history and the apparent triumph of liberal democracy spreads around the globe, the domestic state of democracy within the United States continues to erode. Rather than a nation where citizens feel empowered in their common governance, the United States has become a land where the vast majority of citizens hate their leaders yet never vote. Massive anti-incumbency sentiments and resentment toward representative government have paralleled the rise of grassroots militia movements and media demagogues. Clearly something has gone wrong with democracy in the United States—or more precisely, with the way democracy is understood and exercised.

Nowhere are these difficulties more pronounced than in battles over cultural issues. Debates about canonical values, revisionist curricula, artistic censorship, and freedom of expression have moved from the margins of public debate to its center. Increasingly, people across the political spectrum recognize the strategic role of communication media in shaping human identities and influencing politics. At a historic moment lacking in superpower conflicts, ideological debate has become internalized as it did in the 1950s. Once again battles that were waged with guns and bullets are now fought with ideas and symbols. And once again access to the debate is a crucial issue, as attempts are made to exclude voices that would contest the status quo.

Increasingly in recent years the debates about the content and character of contemporary democracy turn to technology. As in the discourse of education, technology and the new forms of communication it enables are regarded by many as a means of leveling social inequities and erasing problematic differences. Much as Marshall McLuhan forecasted a "global village" wired like the human nervous system in which instantaneous communications would prevent misunderstanding and conflict, proponents of the

Internet and its related technologies suggest that cyberspace will exercise a magical cure for a plethora of social ills. As Al Gore has put it, "Our new ways of communicating will entertain as well as inform. More importantly, they will educate, promote democracy, and save lives."[1]

Such rhetoric constitutes yet another way in which cyberspace is credited with utopian powers to generate insight, connectedness, and prosperity, and at the same time to allow us to forget or deny the forces that mitigate against equality, community, and social justice. Overlooked in this discourse are the many ways that technology is used by government, corporations, and individuals for purposes ranging from surveillance to profiteering. Indeed the promotion of virtual communities and cyberdemocracy frequently is little more than another way in which technology becomes abstracted from the human relations surrounding it and romanticized as an autonomous force. This tendency was recognized by Theodore Rozak while the Internet was being developed two decades ago. Rozak wrote that "information technology has the obvious capacity to concentrate political power, to create new forms of social obfuscation and domination."[2]

The Virtual Community

In recent years it has become commonplace to discuss the Internet as a community—as a virtual place where people meet, chat, conduct business, and develop a sense of togetherness. The dictionary definition of *community* describes "a unified body of individuals," people "living in a particular area," or in the more general sense, "a body of persons or nations having a common history or common social, economic, or political interests."[3] Hence it is important to stress that even in its most generic definitions, *community* is conceived as a relationship among people as much as a place. Long before the Internet existed as an idea, researchers looking at community had realized its function as a "network" made possible by mail, telephones, automobiles, and such mass communications media as television and movies. With this in mind, Raymond Williams wrote that "the process of communication is in fact the process of community."[4]

This idea of community as an intellectual construct was elaborated by Benedict Anderson in his 1980s formulation of the "imagined community."[5] To Anderson, the very way that people view themselves as members of a group or citizens of a nation hinges on an imaginative leap enabled by common association, but reinforced by such entities as news and entertainment media. As Anderson described it, "All communities larger than primordial villages of face-to-face contact (and perhaps even these) are imagined. Communities are to be distinguished, not by their falsity or genuineness, but by the style in which they are imagined."[6] In more recent years, linguistic scholars have described speech communities, interpretive communities, and other types of "virtual communities" from fan clubs to mail art groups enabled by understandings that generate relations of inclusion and exclusion. In other words the idea of virtual communities, so celebrated as a revolutionary concept by Internet technophiles, is nothing new. To scholars like Manuel Castells, the virtual community also offers little of consequence aside from the way it throws traditional concepts of community into relief. Castells writes that "the opposition between 'real' and 'imagined' communities is of little analytical use beyond the laudable effort at demystifying ideologies of essentialist nationalism."[7]

In this context, the idea of communities enabled by the Internet hardly seems like a great insight. Yet the online manifestation of the "virtual community" has generated a powerful mythos in the popular mind. Why is this so? The simple answer is that apparent technological novelty has once again been promoted successfully as a revolutionary force. In an era of wireless Web access and proliferating e-commerce, community is simply another part of life that has become digitized and thereby improved. But on another level, the idea of digital connectedness resonates powerfully at a time when many people feel alienated and estranged from public life. The network begins to appear as a viable option when "real" communities are diminishing and people feel more powerless. Is it any wonder that the tremendous popularity of Internet communities is growing at a time when the majority of citizens no longer participate in electoral politics, when corporate mergers and monopoly business practices are at an all-time high, and when social service networks both here and abroad are all but dismantled? Factor in such historical changes as the weakening of organized labor and religion, the moral bankruptcy of party politics, changes in the traditional family structure, the declining role of the state—and the state is set for something "new" to capture the public imagination. As Joseph Lockard has written, "virtual communities, in short have become a new governing myth. The opening of new communications paradigms coincides with a yawning and unfulfilled need for community."[8] Despite the irony that the Internet's "data commerce" transmission capability is what enables corporate consolidation and multinational capitalism, people are drawn to electronic means of communal intimacy.

Some attribute this yearning for community to the proliferation of an image world that seems to replace material experience at every turn. Guy Debord asserts that "there is no place left where people can discuss the realities which concern them, because they can never lastingly free themselves from the crushing presence of media discourse."[9] This certainly is a major theme in the writing of Jean Baudrillard, who sees "electronic communication as part of the whole web of hyper-realistic illusion we've turned to, in our technologically stimulated flight from the breakdown of human communities."[10] In this regard the virtual community offers first and foremost a way of being with others, and secondarily a novel way of controlling that association by bracketing it in time and space: community on demand, at the touch of a switch, from the distance of a remote screen.

An unabashed advocate of the social potentials of these "virtual" encounters, Howard Rheingold asserts that life in cyberspace is virtually identical to life in physical space, except "we leave our bodies behind."[11] It goes without saying that the virtual crowd also leaves behind such bodily inconveniences as hunger, poverty, and violence in the pursuit of electronic comradeship. Yet in a vision of simulated experience worthy of William Gibson, Rheingold sees the gap between virtual faction and physical reality shortening. As he puts it,

> Not only do I inhabit my virtual communities; to the degree that I carry around their conversations in my head and begin to mix it up with them in real life, my virtual communities also inhabit my life. I've been colonized; my sense of family at the most fundamental level has been virtualized.[12]

This is where things get interesting. Rather than focusing on the binary opposition of virtual/nonvirtual worlds (or to put it another way, representation and reality) these two spheres can be viewed as mutually informing. Each reflects and shapes the other. In this sense the notion of a virtual community need not be regarded so much as an end in itself, but rather as one of many "spaces" where dialogues can emerge. *Whole Earth Catalogue* founder Stewart Brand describes the virtual meeting place as much like the public sphere.

> There's always another mind there. It's like having the corner bar, complete with old buddies and delightful newcomers and new tools waiting to take home and fresh graffiti and letters, except instead of putting on my coat, shutting down the computer, and walking to the corner, I just invoke my telecom program and there they are. It's a place.[13]

For obvious reasons, the idea of virtual communities has become attractive in certain political circles. This was the fundamental premise behind Ross Perot's vision of national "electronic town meetings" for conducting instantaneous votes on public policy issues—an idea later advocated by Newt Gingrich and former Clinton adviser Dick Morris. This notion of a giant national conversation holds enormous popular appeal, for it satisfies both the affective desire for an inclusive community and the "commonsense" thinking that such a unified common culture is possible and advisable.

Of course, the very premise of elected "representation" was intended in part as a buffer against the faddish indulgences of unbridled populism. Indeed, Washington's current reliance on focus groups and instant polls provoked a writer in *Time* to comment that the federal government "isn't dangerously disconnected from the people; the trouble may be it's too plugged in."[14] These sentiments are echoed by Jonathan Gill, special projects coordinator for the White House Office of Media Affairs, who is particularly leery of the growing media frenzy over making democratic decisions in cyberspace. Gill fears that such capacities may in fact do more harm than good if not deployed with restraint. "Democracy requires dialogue, reflection, learning, growth, and the ability to evolve," Gill recently wrote, adding, "all of which require time and not channel-clicking."[15]

The idea of electronic town meetings faded over time as an overt means of determining public policy, as the Internet has come to be used more as a publicity and polling instrument. At the same time, criticism has begun to grow about the ability of the Internet to create communities as well as the manner in which communities are sustained online. From some quarters have come complaints of the Internet's "artificiality" in offering but a phantom version of collective experience. As Shawn Wilbur writes, "Virtual community is the illusion of community where there are no real people and no real community. It is a term used by idealistic technophiles, who fail to understand that the authentic cannot be engendered through technical means."[16] Although it is possible to dismiss this critique as an essentialist yearning for an elusive "real" flesh-and-blood community, the fact remains that little in the way of traditional organizing has taken place on the Internet. Dave Healy asserts that "true community on the Internet is threatened by non-instrumentality" because online initiatives rarely lead to action in the offline world, except in instances of a perceived threat to the autonomy of the Net itself, such as the overstated danger posed by the proposed Clipper chip.[17] The logic of these critiques lies in the apparent ease in which Internet associations are made and the resultant lack of commitment among those who make them.

This is not to say that the Internet is without its communal effects. Those who say that online worlds have little "real" effect often discount the growing significance of the Internet as its own world and the subsequent impact that world is having. On one level, the Internet has become a prodigious medium of commerce—initial overstatements notwithstanding—in the form of such entities as Amazon.com, E-toys, and various software, video and MP3 music outlets. Such corporations certainly have recognized the power of "community" as a way of developing and organizing cohorts of customers. The interactive capabilities of Amazon's Web site allow it to analyze information on a customer's purchases to produce a continually changing set of "recommendations" for new purchases. These are accompanied by "customer reviews" and lists such as "Customers who bought this book also bought books by. . . ." This creates a simulation of a community of readers with similar interests—all generated by a computer. Other retailers promote community via special gatherings announced through e-mail invitations, or print publications that one receives as a supplement to online services, or memberships in "priority" clubs or discount buyers' groups. All of this is done in the interest of instilling a sense of affiliation, brand loyalty, or "membership." As Jeremy Rifkin explains, "There's a growing awareness among management and marketing experts alike that establishing so-called communities of interest is the most effective way to capture and hold customer attention and create lifetime relationships."[18]

While this might sound like simply another form of commodification, the transformation of community into a commercial product has serious implications. The way people form communities says a great deal about the way they understand themselves and their world. It also has a great deal to do with the way people communicate and their ability to do so. Rifkin asserts that "because communication is the means by which human beings find common meaning and share the world they create, commodifying all forms of digital communication goes hand-in-hand with commodifying the many relationships that make up the lived experience—the cultural life—of the individual and the community."[19]

Although not a political community in the conventional sense, the Internet has been used successfully to mobilize constituencies to write letters and communicate with legislators as well as orchestrate online "demonstrations" resulting from mass e-mailings to single sites. On another level, the Internet's impact is more accurately interpreted as a function of culture than as material presence. This is well recognized by the growing number of corporations who use the Internet as an advertising medium, not to mention investors who pay inflated rates for shares in Internet companies that make no profits. Like other mass media, the Net is becoming a major conduit for the reflection and manufacture of human desire. Finally, the Internet enables a form of data community in the growing use of tracking and profiling software to surreptitiously collect information on Internet users and to aggregate them into target consumer groups, mailing lists, or simple statistics for analysis. In other words, you belong to online communities regardless of your knowledge or willingness to join.

Cyberdemocracy

How do these contradictory forms of Internet community relate to democracy? Do they offer new forums for public discourse and civic participation, as is often suggested? Or do they simply refashion old forms of democracy with a new face? The overarching question in this regard is whether it is possible for a technology to create new political structures or understandings of political life, without changing the fundamental power structures and social organizations in which the technology operates. Does the Internet have the capability of changing the way people conceive their relations to one another? If so, is it ever possible for such new understandings to escape the historical and cultural baggage from which they emerge? Or is it more likely that the most new technologies offer is an improved way of addressing the world as it exists?

When entertaining the prospect of democracy it is necessary from the outset to acknowledge its problematic modernist underpinnings. Born of an enlightenment vision of rationality and a collective common sense, traditional democracy presumes the existence of an autonomous subjectivity capable of a liberating escape from superstition, aristocratic oligarchy, totalitarianism, and ultimately, history itself. This does not jibe well with postmodern formulations of the contingent subject, continually shaped and influenced by language, experience, and social structure. Nor does democracy square well in the context of an online world in which identities are disbursed, partial, and often distorted, disguised, or false.

Often evoked in discussions of online democracy is the "public sphere" as articulated by Jürgen Habermas. Through critiques of Habermas's original model, one can begin to formulate alternative versions of modernist democracy. Before the existence of modern telecommunications, the print era afforded citizens unrelated by physical geography, native ethnicity, or religious tradition an enhanced experience of a mutual culture and shared a perception of nationality. The resulting respect for published forums prompted the framers of the U.S. Constitution and the French Declaration of the Rights to legislate journalistic freedom. As James Madison wrote, "The People shall not be deprived or abridged of their Right to speak, to write, or to publish their sentiments; and the Freedom of the Press, as one of the great Bulwarks of Liberty, shall be inviolable."[20]

This desire for a free press developed from a number of specific historical conditions. Politically, these convictions emerged from fears that an all-powerful state might exert influence over the precious medium of print. Philosophically, early free speech arguments grew from the Enlightenment belief (shared by many contemporary anti-censorship advocates) that individuals could resist external influence in making autonomous personal judgments. Socially, free speech was premised on the faith that existing communications media could adequately convey the views of all citizens.

The idealized space in which this "free and open" communication would occur has been labeled by Habermas the "bourgeois public sphere."[21] According to Habermas,

> By "public sphere" we mean first of all a domain of our social life in which such a thing as public opinion can be formed. Access to the public sphere is open in principle to all citizens. A portion of the public sphere is constituted in every conversation in which private persons come together to form a public. They are then acting neither as business or professional people conducting their private affairs, nor as legal associates subject to the legal regulations of state bureaucracy and obligated to obedience. Citizens act as a public when they deal with matters of general interest without being subject to coercion; thus with the guarantee that they may assemble and unite freely; and express and publicize their opinions freely.[22]

It's important to stress that the public sphere was never an achievable fact, but an idealized horizon. To Habermas, a key analytical question of contemporary social analysis has become one of accounting for the growing discrepancy between the conceptual frame of the public sphere and actual social relations. In historical actuality, while certain venues occasionally offered relatively open spaces for the common exchange of views and the testing of civic arguments, they couldn't provide a perfect incubator for democracy. No public medium has ever provided a completely unmediated conduit of civic discourse. Nor has any public sphere been capable of compensating for the differing backgrounds, perceptions, and social locations of those entering it. Moreover, despite assertions of "universal rights" by its early proponents, the public sphere never did much for those kept out—which in the Enlightenment era meant women, slaves, and immigrants.

The horizon of a public sphere receded further into the distance near the end of the nineteenth century, as the democratic aspirations of liberal philosophy became subverted by advanced capitalism. Technology played an important role. Emergent forms of audio and visual communication helped create myriad new delivery contexts, each with its own reception characteristics. Such developments were accompanied by shifting approaches to commerce based on advertising and public relations, which further complicated the style and function of mass communication. Some analysts attribute to these changes a corresponding loss of agency within the population at large, as citizens began to see themselves less as participants in the ongoing drama of democracy than as observers of its effects.[23] Others see media technologies as enhancements to democracy, which provide more opportunities for viewers to exchange messages and engage in common decision-making.[24]

Either way, within this technological transition the growth of electronic media produced the most profound consequences. With the declining readerships of the newspaper—what Walter Lippman called the "bible of democracy"—radio and television stations became the principal means through which political discourse flowed to the public.[25] Though primarily owned by commercial interests, during the 1930s and 1940s the airwaves carried a relatively broad range of opinion because so much of network time remained unsponsored. With the gradual rise of commercial advertising in the 1950s and 1960s, the potential to influence programming increased. Yet regulatory protections helped insulate this electronic discourse from direct manipulation until decades later. This was largely due to governmental efforts—notably through the Federal Communication Commission—to maintain this public sphere as a civic "trust."

When the Reagan administration assumed power, it effected historic shifts in the democratic function of media through a series of deregulatory measures that aided network consolidation of ownership, increased the role of advertisers and corporate sponsors, and loosened rules of public accountability. With the economic downturns of the late 1980s and early 1990s, the role of market forces grew with budget cutbacks in broadcast journalism, as well as the concomitant rise of government spokespeople and corporate publicists. More recently, the Republican majority in Congress has begun to extend deregulation into the cable and telephone industries, a move that could have a devastating effect on the democratic potential of the information superhighway.[26]

As the public sphere has been assaulted politically it also has been critiqued theoretically. Perhaps the most fundamental critique, highly applicable to the Internet, lies in Habermas's idealization of a public sphere of free and open access to all. As with other forms of communication media, the uneven distribution of Internet access invalidates much of its claim as a "public" vehicle for democratic debate. In a similar way, contemporary feminists have pointed out that the overriding application of the public sphere in terms of conventionally defined "public" communications unfairly excludes forms of exchange typically consigned to the private. Initially referring to the domestic sphere, this concern for "private" communication becomes of increasing concern as so many functions of government are being transferred to the "private" sector.

Problematic as well is the way in which "consensus" is formulated. Here individual and constituent group subjectivity figures prominently, as the consensus accord asks participants to simultaneously advance their common interests and surrender differences. Invariably, the suppression of variance to the majoritarian accord elides the interests of those who fall outside. This led Nancy Fraser to suggest that rather than a single public sphere, it would be better to think of multiple public spheres or "counter-public spheres" that do not call for universal principles to represent all members.

Postmodern Subjects

Given these problems with conventional models of democracy and the public sphere, how does one begin to formulate models of civic participation on the Internet? If postmodernism has taught us anything, it is that formerly sacrosanct domains of knowledge can be questioned and that our interactions with each other can be modified as a consequence. Specifically, postmodernism posits a subject unlike the modernist democratic model of a singular, rational, consensus-driven self—and more in keeping with the multivalent and fluid model called for by the critics of the singular public spheres. Mark Poster, among others, sees this vision of subjectivity embodied in the Internet:

> Technologically determined effects derive from a broad set of assumptions in which what is technological is a configuration of materials that affect other materials, and the relation between technology and human being is external, that is, where human beings are understood to manipulate the materials for ends that they impose upon the technology from a preconstituted position of subjectivity. But what the Internet technology imposes is a dematerialization of communication and in many of its aspects a transformation of the subject position of the individual who engages within it. The Internet resists the basic conditions for asking the question of the effects of technology."[27]

It is important to note that Poster's analysis stops short of suggesting the complete transformation of the subject, as asserted by technological essentialists like Richard Lanham and George Landow, who fall prey to the tendency to literalize theories never intended for such literalization. Nevertheless such formulations hold importance in their ability to convey the way technologies like the Internet can be understood and used by agents with postmodern subjectivity. Rather than masters of or servants to the technology, these subjects exist in a reciprocal relationship with it. Significant in this regard is the level of interactivity the Internet allows, a characteristic that lies at the heart of a functioning democracy. Moreover, as Sandy Stone has pointed out, the Internet's ability to mingle personal choices and expression with those external means that "the distinction between inside and outside has been erased and along with it, the possibility of privacy."[28]

Democracies in Context

Before proceeding further in this discussion of the democratic potentials of cyberspace, it is important to delineate in some detail the various forms of democracy that all too often become subsumed into a single term. In the spirit of those who have questioned the premise of a single public sphere, it is necessary to question singular definitions of *democracy*. In fact, *democracy* is a relative term. Like any other expression, its meaning is a matter of interpretation, debate, and contest—and in recent years it is a word we have heard a great deal: from the "democratic" protests in Tiananmen Square, to the democratic reforms throughout eastern Europe, to "Operation Restore Democracy" in Haiti. While rival ideologies seem ever more flawed and uncertain, evidence abounds of the so-called triumph of liberal democracy. As a term nearly synonymous with the foreign policy objectives of the United States government, democracy has witnessed the fall of many who once vowed to stand in its way. Perhaps not so coincidentally, it is also nearly always equated with the global economic order of market capitalism.

These apparent contradictions in U.S. democracy suggest more than a simple gap between theory and practice. They signify the profoundly fictional character that the democratic ideal has assumed in the public mind. The very slipperiness of the term has permitted its exploitation by a range of politicians, bureaucrats, and philosophers for purposes ranging from electoral sloganeering to military intervention. For this reason an initial step in the salvaging of participatory politics may well entail an analysis of democracy's crisis of meaning. This entails asking such questions as whether democracy functions primarily as a form of decision-making or an instrument of popular empowerment, whether democracy constitutes an abstract ideal or an achievable goal, or whether democracy emerges from within a group or can be externally imposed.

Such questions begin to suggest that the very idea of a single democracy is a fallacy. Instead democracy serves as a marker for a variety of interests, philosophies, and political programs expressed in the continual flux of labels like direct democracy, liberal democracy, juridical democracy, associative democracy, socialist democracy, and radical democracy, among numerous others. At the same time, these questions throw into relief the way democracy has become essentialized as an undefined norm—joining such ambiguous expressions as "mainstream opinion" and "family values," which lack a clear definition yet are highly effective in discrediting selected groups. It is therefore in the interest of "democratic" ideals to attempt to unpack the various discourses of democracy.

One way of envisioning democracy is at the end of a participatory continuum, the other end of which marks the complete exclusion of people from their common decision making. Yet contrary to much contemporary rhetoric, even this simple view of democracy also implies a set of limits on human behavior—a series of restraints on freedom itself. Any subscription to democracy presupposes a degree of faith in the possibility of politics—a belief that human need can be addressed within communities, as opposed to the anarchy of absolute privacy, liberty, and individualism. Put this way, debates over different forms of democracy boil down to arguments over what kind of common compacts are desirable or possible in a given society.

Like other social formations, democracy is enabled by the agents of the populous who call it into being. Classical theory located this agency in the category of the citizen, bound in a contractual relationship with the state to cede certain freedoms for corresponding rights. The exact terms of this contract vary with the form of democracy used. In direct or "pure" democracies, citizens engage in common decision making without the mediation of a legislature or other representative body. Such democratic structures originated on nearly every continent, although the first written records of such practices are commonly attributed to the ancient Greeks. This privileging of Athenian democracy over other "preliterate" models has become a matter of no small consequence, in its historic deployment to assert the primacy of Western civilization and to justify its "natural" posture of dominance.

Related to these questions about representation are similar debates about the fairness of majority rule. Classical participatory theory holds that although decisions are made in winner-take-all voting, the regularity of polling ensures that no majority is permanent. If any agreement proves inadequate it will be overturned in a subsequent ballot. For this reason, any majority has reason to remain sensitive to the needs of the minority. In practice, however, majorities have often used their political leverage to maintain their dominance. Commentators from Alexis de Tocqueville to Lani Guinier have criticized this fundamental precept of democracy for its inability to fairly represent all citizens.[29] The frequently evoked concept of the "tyranny of the majority" results, not only from winner-take-all electoral systems, but from the persistent failure of democracies to enfranchise potential voters without discrimination.

Critiques of this essentialized view of democracy often begin by pointing to the internal contradictions of Athenian society. Although credited with the "invention" of democracy, ancient Greece permitted only one social group access to this sanctified realm. All members of society may have had equal and unmediated participation in civic life, but women, slaves, and non-Greeks were excluded from the fraternity of citizenship. Far from a mere historical "problem" in classical democracy, this very issue of who counts as a voting citizen has plagued Western democracies ever since. It is important to point out that even within the United States—the purported model of world democracy—such a fundamental issue as women's suffrage was contested well into the twentieth century. Even these advances remained in question in such purportedly enlightened nations as Germany, Italy, and Spain, where the right to vote was systematically withheld from certain groups for subsequent decades. The denial of voting rights within the United States to African Americans and other immigrant groups remained a point of severe acrimony through the 1950s and 1960s. Problems with other immigrant groups persist even today.

Despite these problems, Athenian direct democracy retains relevance for many as a philosophical ideal. The notion of active citizenship as a defining principle of public life informs many contemporary debates over issues ranging from radical pluralism to communitarianism. Indeed contemporary exhortations about "public service" in the name of the "national family" emanate from a nostalgic yearning for a preliberal sense of civic responsibility. At issue is the degree to which direct democracy or active citizenship can be realized in massive postindustrial societies. Such idealized political models flourished in the relatively immobile atmospheres of small, oral societies in which face-to-face meetings constituted an organic part of daily life. But as European society became more complex, so did its forms of democracy. With the rise of the Roman Empire, the era of classical Italian republicanism marked a transition to elected leadership, and along with it the beginning of a gradual distancing of civic governance from the citizenry. Rome's mixed government, with its interlocking system of consuls and people's tribunals, became a model for an intermediate form of democracy—in which the people remained the ultimate source of accountability, but in which forms of representation became a necessity.

The ethical dimensions of this transition from direct democracy cannot be overstated, for the shift to representative forms of government signaled a weakening of the sense of individual responsibility in community governance. The profound influence of the Christian church in the Middle Ages displaced secular morality as a motivation for involved citizenship. The prospect of divine reward helped undermine any sense of urgency about earthly problems. At the same time religion helped foster forms of community identification that would ultimately become a separate territory of civic life. As a result, the increasingly atomized quality of secular society called for new forms of political organization that could accommodate and contain individualism and competition.

Liberal democracy evolved in direct response to the perceived encroachment of the state on personal liberty. At the center of the liberal democratic ethos lies the Western notion of the autonomous individual, capable of free choice and motivated by capitalistic self-interest. Most important is the separability of existence into public and private domains. The public comprises the arena of laws, legislatures, and other civic structures, whose ultimate logic is reducible to an apolitical ideal of the common good.[30] The formation of a disinterested and distinct public sphere reveals the uniquely Western belief in Cartesian epistemology—a belief in the possibility of a knowable independent ground apart from humanity's base instincts. The transcendental universalism of the public sphere is the antithesis of the self-interested specificity of the private realm of personal interests and market competition.

The unifying element for many liberal democratic theorists is belief that individual interest can be enhanced by mutual cooperation. As John Locke put it, "The great and chief end therefore of men uniting into commonwealths and putting themselves under government . . . is the mutual preservation of their lives, liberties, and estates, which we shall call by the general name property."[31] This impulse for accumulation is both enabled and limited by the state. Hence, liberal democracy assumes a two-stroke function as a justification and limit for the exercise of state authority. Regular elections serve the philosophical goal of obliging the public to clarify public issues while ensuring that no government or set of public officials would remain in office forever.

Opinions differ among liberal democrats over how much the consensus should apply to all citizens. This is both the rationale for local government and the reasoning behind various pluralist versions of liberal democracy. Pluralists agree that different groups deserve different degrees of influence over various matters according to the proportion of their interest in them. Within the liberal logic of self-interest, people are more likely to exercise their agency as citizens over matters that affect them most directly.

This principle has led some liberals to advocate a strengthening of the civil society as a means of decentralizing democracy and lessening the role of the state. The civil society argument, occasionally termed the *associationalist* view, asserts that the goals of social justice and human welfare are best served by voluntary and self-governing private bodies, such as unions, political parties, religious organizations, schools, neighborhood groups, clubs, and societies.[32] This position gained popularity in the Western world during the nineteenth century, but was squeezed out of existence with the growing dominance of collectivist and individualist politics. Although similar to liberal democracy, this view differs in according voluntary bodies a primary role in organizing social life, rather than an ancillary function to government. These smaller, private entities, which may or may not be governed by democratic principles, are viewed as more flexible and responsive to community needs. Representative government assumes a regulatory function as guarantor of services, rather than acting as their provider. Limited to this oversight role, government bureaucracy is lessened and its efficiency enhanced as a consequence.

A related trend has been the growing popularity of communitarianism, in which the ethical dimensions of voluntarism are emphasized over the mandates of self-interest. As espoused by Amitai Etzioni and William Gallston, the trouble with conventional liberalism is that it focuses too much on individual rights and not enough on shared values.[33] To overcome these problems, communitarians suggest that people should become more involved in developing the "social glue" that holds society together through such entities as schools, neighborhoods, and the family. The communitarian emphasis on the traditional nuclear family, in particular, has drawn the fire of those who claim that communitarianism masks a traditionalist agenda. Others have faulted the doctrine's cultural and microinstitutional approach, arguing that social problems like structural unemployment and entrenched racism cannot be addressed strictly on an interpersonal level.

If democracy is conceptualized as a series of compromises between individual and collective interest, socialist democracy clearly leans in the latter direction. Critical of the liberal emphasis on competition, Karl Marx and Friedrich Engles viewed material inequities, not merely as by-products of such a model, but necessary components of it. To create winners in the game of acquisition, a system must also generate losers. The much ballyhooed "opportunities" for liberty offered by liberal capitalism mean little if they are not universally accessible. The inequities produced by capital in turn spoil the very functioning of democracy, as the state becomes little more than a tool of the privileged. In this scheme the very idea of a separation between private and public is thrown into question. Rather than serving as an idealized and apolitical mediator of the common good, government is perverted by the ability of some citizens to exert more control over it than others.

Applications of socialist democracy vary greatly. The formula commonly offered is the merger of the government with private institutions to eliminate any advantages held. Within this logic preoccupations with individual liberty become irrelevant, as do assertions of groups claiming rights on the basis of identity. Social inequities are perceived primarily as economic matters, resolvable by the dissolution of capitalism. Consequently, as the social hierarchies of class distinction are eradicated, the need for personal autonomy is diminished. Individual freedom becomes a redundancy in a society where all needs of the citizenry are addressed. This principle compels some to argue that an ideal socialist society by definition constitutes a democracy.

Like liberal democracy, the principles of socialist democracies have suffered somewhat in practical application. As demonstrated by the Soviet Union and other nations of the eastern European bloc, difficulties emerged in the capacities of single-party bureaucracies to remain responsive to local constituencies. This anti-democratic drive to single-party agreement and conformity was worsened by the development over time of a managerial class of party bureaucrats and government officials. Moreover, the structure of state ownership of property has the effect of denying resources to oppositional groups. The ability to mount political alternatives to the state, while not completely foreclosed by a socialist system, is significantly hampered. Not unlike the elite-driven governments of the West, many socialist democracies evolved structures similarly distanced from popular rule.

The post-World War II atmosphere of growing Cold War tension eventually produced a range of efforts to ameliorate antagonisms between liberal and socialist democrats.[34] Not surprisingly, these hybrid democracies differ considerably. One of the most significant distinctions lies in the degree to which these hybrids emphasize material or cultural matters. The materialist camp is exemplified by the work of John Dunn, Samuel Bowles, and Herbert Gintis, who focus on the system of inequities of capitalism in their calls for economic democracy (what Bowles and Gintis term *postliberal* democracy).[35] These authors argue that democracy emerges from the participatory management of property and production. Unlike traditional socialists who advocate the centralized organization of this authority, economic democrats typically favor more heterogeneous sites of power, where decisions can be made by constituencies identified by rights claims.

In contrast to economic democracy, the culturalist solution to the liberalism/socialism divide argues that capitalism will be undone by enhanced civic participation itself. Once people understand the potentials of equality in one sphere, they will attempt to extend into every other area of life. This approach to politics was codified by Norberto Bobbio, who was strongly influenced by the populist sentiments of Antonio Gramsci. Although critical of the inequities inherent in liberal capitalism, Bobbio saw the modernist assertion of individual agency as a social force that was too powerful to be undone. To accommodate the values of freedom and equality, Bobbio proposed a strongly constitutional democracy, in which competitive parties would represent constituent interests. The importance of the party stemmed from a perception of a society too diverse to achieve a single "common sense." Setting this form of politics apart from typical representative democracies would be a series of compacts designed to block what Bobbio termed the "invisible powers" of industry and finance from exerting undue influence. To achieve this citizens would not simply be given equal "political rights," but also equal "social rights" to ensure that their political rights would suffer no interference.

Central to Bobbio's thinking was a reorientation of the conventional distinction between "public" and "private" realms. Loosely speaking, these terms separate human activity into categories of general and particular concern—with the latter typically considered "off limits" to political discussion. As Bobbio and others subsequently came to believe, this separation has created a dangerous trade-off, as so-called public decision-making increasingly takes on a life of its own and becomes distanced from the daily lives of the citizenry. To remedy the situation, the means of political representation need to be spread further into the basic fabric of daily life: work, education, leisure, and the home. As Bobbio explained in a famous quotation, the problem of democracy is no longer "who votes," but "where one votes."[36]

In the contemporary United States, this distancing of the general from the particular has become manifest in a broad-based suspicion among voters of public officials and the anti-incumbency sentiments that led to massive congressional overhaul in the 1994 elections. In that circumstance, opportunistic conservatives successfully exacerbated public anxieties about a federal government grown too large and intrusive. As in other instances the conventional solution to the public/private dilemma has been to place increased emphasis on local ballots, in which communities need not acquiesce to general social mandates. Regrettably, this solution has proven ineffective in serving the needs of diverse groups—such as those defined by age, gender, occupation, race, ethnicity, or sexual orientation—within and across geographical communities. This dilemma has led certain theorists to advocate an enhanced emphasis on pluralism, with approaches ranging from a reassertion of the civil society to more radical prescriptions.

Twentieth-century pluralist arguments in the West can be traced to the liberal discontent with state centrism, exacerbated by the increasing social diversification and class stratification brought on by industrialization. Groups in Europe and the United States began to argue that the liberal dyad of individual and state insufficiently represented the complexity of civil subjectivity. Needed was a way of accounting for the more complex differentiation of individuals into groups and identities. The emphasis on locating a "middle ground" between state authority and individual autonomy was further tempered by an antagonism toward what C. Wright Mills termed "the power elite"—a hegemonic class of business interests perceived to dominate capitalist society. Despite this apparent awareness of the tendency of private interests to impinge upon and influence the public functions of government, most U.S. pluralist thinking of this period did little to question conventional demarcations between the two. In other words, although postwar pluralism failed to recognize the permeability of the categories public and private, it failed to see this as more than a structural problem. Instead it sought to promote the interests of diverse groups by pushing private interests back in their place as equal competitors, hence rebuttressing the public/private divide.

To subsequent poststructuralist theorists this move did little more than reinscribe the notion of the modernist subject. Not only did the postwar U.S. pluralists reinforce conventional public/private categories, but they also were incapable of recognizing the subjects of politics as anything other than members of discrete groups. Postwar pluralism marked a significant advance over unreconstructed liberalism in carving out a larger role and a more complex arena for citizens to act politically, but it only did so within existing understandings of citizens' roles. Theorists such as Ernesto Laclau and Chantal Mouffe proposed what they termed a "radical democratic" reconceptualization of the citizen unencumbered by essentialist categories of modernist subjectivity. Far from a unified and autonomous member of a particular constituency, within this formulation each person belongs to numerous overlapping groups and multiple intersecting identities. As Mouffe explains, "It is not a matter of establishing a mere alliance between given interests but of actually modifying their identity to bring about a new political identity."[37] As this group-identification model ties its subjects irrevocably to the social, individuality is also maintained because of the relatively unique mix of association within each person.

This radical democratic model of the subject has profound implications for political organization, for it shatters convenient distinctions between public and private. As speculated by Kirstie McClure, this formulation could imply a reinscription of the "subject of rights" that implies not so much an escape from the state, nor an "abdication from political participation more conventionally understood, but rather a potential refusal of a unitary construct of citizenship as exhaustive of the political tasks of the present."[38] This reformulation of the subject need not be understood as a simple collapse of former private concerns into the public arena, or vice versa. According to Laclau and Mouffe, this should be seen instead as an opportunity for the creation of "new political spaces."[39] In the expanded view of the multiple subject, the very definition of the political becomes broadened to a new range of sites beyond the conventional jurisdiction of state institutions into the far more dynamic domain of cultural representations and social practices.

In such a context, this poststructuralist approach to pluralism does not negate subjective agency as it is often accused of doing. Instead, by opening new territory for scrutiny the model gives new vitality to the impetus for democratic principles. The politicization of formerly social spaces formerly considered neutral makes apparent the often unacknowledged power relations in everyday activities. In this way such "off-limits" territories as culture, education, and the family become sites of critical investigation and emancipatory contestation. Rather than diminishing a sense of political agency by negating essential notions of the subject, the principles of the radical democracy have the potential of reinvigorating the subject within new domains of influence. Just as important, in arguing against the notion of a fixed or universal subject, the project of a radical democracy is, by definition, never complete.

Despite their utopian aspirations (perhaps because of them), prescriptions for radical pluralism have been subject to strenuous critique. Many on the left assert that a focus on identity and on definitions of the subject tends to minimize the importance of economic issues and the particulars of social structure.[40] Radical democracy may promise an egalitarian program but does little to spell out the details of how it will address redistributive issues. This lack of specificity is similarly critiqued from postcolonial quarters as one indication that this purportedly "postmodern" approach to politics simply may constitute another brand of modernism in disguise. In this critique radical pluralism's failure to articulate where and how its program will be implemented is interpreted as a universalizing impulse that refused to acknowledge social inequalities. The general "right" of citizens to vote is undermined by the absence of other privileges that such universalizing rhetoric obscures. Without acknowledging the ethnocentric and otherwise xenophobic character of these absences, radical democracy becomes simply "the latest" chapter in an enlightenment program of Western advancement. Evidence of this evolutionary view comes, for example, from radical democracy's preservation and adaptation of liberal principles. Due to this allegiance to the liberal legacy, still other critics claim that radical democracy represents little more than a new name devised by disaffected socialists, who are drifting toward liberal democracy but who can't bring themselves to embrace it.

Regardless of the brand of democracy one prefers, the proliferation of democratic societies around the globe is abundantly evident—although the precise meaning of this proliferation is difficult to gauge. Clearly in certain contexts this democratic globalization is far from an innocent or "natural" occurrence, as democracy is deployed to mask foreign intervention and neocolonial expansionism. In other situations these changes seem more benign. Either way, this global extension of democracy can become a way of envisioning political relations—not merely *within* nations, but *among* them as well. This concept of a global democracy becomes especially important in light of the growing concentration of economic relations across sovereign borders. As Noam Chomsky put it, "A de facto world government, led by transnational corporations is now taking place," composed of the International Monetary Fund, the World Bank, the G-7, General Agreement on Tariffs and Trade and other structures promoting a "new imperial age."[41]

Cyberdemocracy

Given the identification of Internet providers and computer manufacturers as multinational corporations fully participating in the inequitable distribution of informational technology worldwide, it seems unlikely that cyberspace will bring about the democratization of the globe anytime soon. Once again, the essentially expansionist character of the capitalistic enterprise cannot be overstated. It is the single most powerful characteristic of contemporary technological society and it is ruthless in its drive. The historical roots of this ethos are described by Ziauddin Sardar in the introduction of one of the only books addressing global techno-colonialism in the digital age: *Cyberfutures: Culture and Politics on the Information Superhighway.*[42] Sardar writes,

> Western civilization has always been obsessed with new territories to conquer. The narratives of the conquests, on the whole, have followed a basic linear pattern. The hunger for new conquests stems from the insatiable desire to acquire new wealth and riches which in turn provides the impetus for the development of new technologies of subjugation. . . . Once the new territory has been colonized, it is handed over to business interests to loot.[43]

This impulse is manifest in the business of information technology, and articulated succinctly in a cover headline appearing in a 1990 issue of *Mondo 2000*, which reads "The Rush Is On! Colonizing Cyberspace."[44] As Sardar explains, the concept of the "frontier," so central to the expansionist agenda, has itself functioned as governing myth that permits invasion and exploitation. "The frontier exists in the mind, it operates as a myth only after the process of control has already been established."[45] Within this logic the "frontier is the agency through which power elites get everyone to do their work while thinking they are acting on their own volition. Cyberspace frontier is no different. It has already been controlled; the populace are now being motivated to explore and settle in the new frontier."[46] Considered in cultural terms, this expansionist Western cyberspace becomes the defining medium for all of the world's peoples—even though the majority of the world's population has no access to it. "Cyberspace is a giant step toward the museumification of the world; where anything remotely different from Western cultures will exist only in digital form. And in digital form, not only their past but also their present and potential futures can be manipulated."⁴⁷ Here it's worth reiterating that the epistemic violence perpetrated on non-Western people and communities of color within the Western world is not a matter of symbolism alone. Practically every video or computer game one can purchase is laden with tropes of discovery, conquest, and xenophobia of one kind or another. One should remember that the technology now used in most games was originally developed for military purposes, a parallel made tragically clear in the media coverage of the Gulf War in which the massacre of thousands by the U.S. military was neutralized by its abstraction into gamelike visual formats.

Within the United States it hardly seems that the Internet will dramatically alter the shape of national democratic debate—as was once prophesied. Despite all claims to the contrary there is nothing inherently democratic or decentralizing about the Internet. Like the telephone, it is a technology that can be used by people with democratic ambitions. And like the telephone, that use can be expensive, exclusive, or simply unavailable for large numbers of people. Worse still, for those who romanticize the Internet as a "naturally" democratic medium, the Net can become little more than a vehicle of political voyeurism. For one thing, the type of community the Net enables is hardly like that in the non-Net worlds. In this regard Sarder asks,

> What responsibilities does the "electronic neighborhood" place on its members? Can one simply resign one's membership from a community? And is identity simply a matter of which electronic newsgroup one belongs to? Communities are shaped by a sense of belonging to a place, a geographical location, by shared values, by common struggles, by tradition and history of a location— not by joining a group with common interests.⁴⁸

Although the Internet offers a kind of community, it is important not to confuse it with more traditional social or political groupings. Cyberspace offers membership in communities more like television audiences or fan clubs than political parties or service organizations.

The critical issue in this simulation of community is the way it suggests that it is something different, thus encouraging people to invest their trust in these new Internet communities. The most significant difference that cyberspace communities embody is their orientation as commercial entities through which access is advertised, metered, and delivered at a price. Although this once might have seemed like an insult to the average citizen, the commercialization of politics has become accepted and expected in an age in which most political speech now reaches voters through advertising rather than any other means. As Manuel Castells has argued, "Electronic media have become the privileged space of politics. . . . Outside the media sphere there is only political marginality."[49] To Castells the larger patterns of declining state legitimacy and the weakening of the civil society of private institutions like labor unions, churches, and civic organizations—along with the now dominant role of media in politics and public life—have created an atmosphere in which citizens are increasingly confused and open to manipulation. Castells writes,

> The blurring of boundaries of the nation state confuses the definition of citizenship. The absence of a clear situs of power dilutes social control and diffuses political challenges. The rise of communalism, in its different forms, weakens the principle of political sharing on which democratic politics is based. The growing inability of the state to control capital flows and ensure social security diminishes its relevance for the average citizen.[50]

The result is a society in which politics and subjective agency become diluted. As Jean Maria Guehenno writes,

> Nowadays, instead of autonomous subjects there are only ephemeral situations, which serve as support to provisional alliances supported by capacities mobilized for each occasion. Instead of a political space, sites of collective solidarity, they are just dominant perceptions, as ephemeral as the interests that manipulate them. There is a simultaneous atomization and homogenization. A society that is endlessly fragmented, without memory and without solidarity, a society that recovers its unity only in the succession of images that the media return to it every week. It is a society without citizens and ultimately, a non-society.[51]

Within this non-society, values like freedom and equality are more likely to be attributed to products than to the moral desires of a people. Vivian Sobchack has discussed cyberdemocracy as a contradictory terrain in which public perceptions of civic "franchise" are divided between notions of voting and political elections on one hand, and commercial franchises like McDonalds and the L.A. Lakers on the other. So successful have advertisers become in grafting images of civic virtue to products that the two are becoming indistinguishable—as in a recent ad for a no-cost Internet service (supported by advertising alone) that proclaims itself to be "The Defender of the Free World." In this world, democracy represents not so much a matter of free and equal participation in a political system as it does the unimpeded ability to shop, chat, and be entertained. As stated in a recent *Wired* editorial, "technology has given us powers with which we can manipulate not only external reality—the physical world—but also, and much more portentously—

ourselves."⁵² Who exactly is this "we"? For readers of publications like *Wired*, it is a group defined by those it excludes. As explained by Gary Chapman,

> If hyperbolic optimism were all that *Wired* represented, it would be a modestly interesting, if sometimes howlingly brainless, gazette of our times. Unfortunately, the magazine and its popularity among the young, urban elite also seem to present something darker. *Wired*'s inside-outside dichotomy has the taint of contempt for the poor and the uneducated, people not using computers now and not likely, in the near future, to find a reason to use them. The disadvantaged haunt *Wired* by their absence, like a negative space that cannot be seen but can be accounted for. *Wired* frequently exhibits resentment toward any kind of civic obligation that might divert resources from life on the net.⁵³

This story doesn't need to be so one-sided. New communication technologies are not yet lost to democracy because they still exist in a fluid state. Although corporations are quickly moving to consolidate their grip on virtual reality, multimedia, and the Internet, spaces for progressive change still exist on many levels. In the most populist terms, cyberspace subversion is carried out by "hackers" who assault the computer networks by cracking access codes, planting viruses, breaking into databases, and stealing network or telephone time. Mostly the work of White middle-class adolescents, hacking constitutes a classic form of negative resistance. Its youthful perpetrators assert themselves against overwhelming sources of authority, while still leaving the structures of that authority in place. Hackers become virtual renegades, who make surface disturbances on the periphery of an industry whose domination they resent but do little to unseat. This form of resistance is very important in articulating the powerlessness felt by individuals increasingly subject to the regulation, surveillance, and control of computer-based information systems. Yet by failing to address the larger issues of class, gender, and race of technological ownership and control, hackers actually reinforce the very authority they oppose. Indeed, rather than seeking anything remotely resembling a democratic social sphere, the discourse of cyberpunks, hackers, or phreakers is more typically that of a self-involved libertarianism which rarely, if ever, interrogates the logic of technology or capitalism. They play by the rules of the system itself. Sobchack explains,

> It is within this conception of American democracy that our present electronic culture emerges and takes form—a conception that, from a critical perspective, can be seen as dialectically grounded in contradiction and potential inequality, and synthesized as a higher and more general level of value as "competition." Thus, there is every reason to expect that a "democratic" electronic culture will manifest itself in the public sphere in a similar dialectical form. Self-contradictory it will be both more and less (not either more or less) liberating, participa-

tory and interactive than was the case with previous, technologically-mediated cultural forms.[54]

But the story doesn't end there. Although cyberspace has the potential for expanding community, it can just as easily restrict it. America Online, the world's largest Internet service provider, makes an appeal to community a central part of its marketing strategy. Not so widely publicized is the extent to which AOL monitors its members' conversations and movements or the fact that 60 percent of AOL members speak only to each other. In this sense, AOL and other Internet communities become electronic versions of the gated enclaves of upscale suburbia. Visit this idealized "space" and it quickly becomes apparent that the dominant subject position is White, heterosexual, and male—with others erased, mocked, or occasionally imitated for dramatic effect. As Joseph Lockard has written, "Cyberspace is unmistakably signed with European Whiteness. Race and ethnicity are simply not up for discussion in cyberspace social theory, and their very absence identifies unsubstantiated presumptions about community."[55] Indeed, in the enormous discourse that has been generated about the Internet, only a handful of articles or books address race or internationalism. While this may be viewed as a simple matter of omission, it can also be seen as an indication of a broader pattern of exclusion. To Lockard, "middle class suburban America, confronted with its diversity on urban streets, has retreated to cyberspace to avoid the otherwise inescapable realities of diversity."[56]

In many ways the metaphoric language of Internet "homesteading" on an "electronic frontier" adds an imperialistic dimension to this impulse to escape into a fanaticized new world. But the new world of cybertechnology is more than a benign diversion, inasmuch as personal electronic homesteading constitutes but a tiny fraction of the business traffic of global communications. Digital technology is what has enabled the establishment of a multinational corporate world, with high-speed data lines carrying business transactions, stock market reports, electronic fund transfers, and millions of other pieces of finance data at a constant pace. Digital media are the lingua franca of global capital—the universal language of money and power—which means that nations and people who are not connected are simply not participants in this economy and are hardly its beneficiaries. Even as proponents of digital democracy predict the imminent connection of everyone in the world to the Internet, the basic fact remains that 80 percent of the world's population has never used a telephone. On one level this means that the limited access to digital media reinforces the divide between the world's rich and poor, between the connected and the unconnected. On another level, this reinforces a disparity in subjectivity and consciousness. Maria Fernandez has written,

At present one cannot disassociate the manufacture and distribution of these technologies from economic profits made in the developed world or from an ongoing process of the colonization of knowledge that began with the book and continued with media such as film and television. . . . These technologies are crucial for the construction of identity in formerly colonized regions since colonized peoples learn about themselves through these forms of knowledge.[57]

Is it possible to reconcile the democratic aspirations of cyberspace with its inegalitarian materiality? Once again, it is important to view digital media as a terrain of struggle rather than an inherently progressive or regressive medium. From this perspective the potential exists for the Internet to extend the radical democratic principles by democratizing daily life in new ways and in new spaces. Although the unequal distribution of Internet resources cannot be denied and the relationship of Internet users to providers is hardly symmetrical, the Net nevertheless permits some degree of equalization among conversants in online public spaces. For many the Internet provides a way for people previously excluded from public discourse to enter it, and in so doing exerts a subversive effect on official knowledge and "expert" opinion. In breaking down the distinction between public and private conversations/spaces, the Internet holds the potential to fulfill Laclau and Mouffe's desire to see democracy inserted into places where it is often not seen. Similarly, while the Internet enables certain forms of subjectivity, it does not guarantee them. One can begin by striving to avoid certain traps. As Poster has written,

> Postmodern theorists have discovered that modern theory's insistence of the freedom of the subject, its compulsive, repetitive inscription into discourse of the sign of the resisting agent, functions to restrict the shape of identity to its modern form, rather than contributing towards emancipation. Postmodern theory, then, must resist ontologizing any form of the subject.[58]

One way of approaching this is by attempting to move beyond the binary tension between individual and community. All too often the impulses of self-interest and collective interest get pitted against each other, with each implying a denial of difference. This results from a homogenous view of community in which variance is suppressed in favor of a ruling common sense. Consistent with the highest principles of radical democracy is the replacement of a consensus model of community with a politics of difference or an ethos of collaboration. The idea is to create a type of "third space" between the individual and the community, which permits a certain fluidity like that proposed by Gilles Deleuze and Felix Guattari in their formulation of the rhizome as a structure that "connects any point with any other point and none of its features necessarily refers to features of the same kind."[59] This model permits a relationship of "radical encounter and collaboration" that de-territorializes and re-territorializes subject, communities, and nations.

How would this come about? In the absence of a robust state apparatus to organize such relationships, the burden falls to the civil society, to schools, libraries, community centers, museums, and other organizations to recognize their role in formulating a social order that encourages a politics of difference without insisting on consensus. Such spaces would recognize that a healthy democracy is a noisy affair, with social compacts continually subject to scrutiny and contestation. Certainly the Internet and other digital technologies offer important means for developing such relations in virtual environments. But once again, extreme caution must be observed to avoid the assumption that such technologies can unproblematically create new social forms. All too often utopian theorists with the best of intentions have invested expectations in new technology, only to find that the underlying social structures have been bypassed or replicated by the technology. Contemporary democracies are not failing because people lack the technical means to communicate or provide feedback. They are failing because people have lost faith in politicians, politics, and public institutions. The challenge is to restore that faith.

Notes

1. Al Gore, as cited in Peter Kollack and Marc A. Smith, *Communities in Cyberspace* (New York and London: Routledge, 1999), 4.

2. Theodore Rozak, as cited in Kollack and Smith, *Communities in Cyberspace,* 4.

3. *Webster's Ninth New Collegiate Dictionary* (Springfield, Mass.: Merriam-Webster, 1987).

4. Raymond Williams, *Television: Technology and Cultural Form* (New York: Schocken Books, 1975), 59.

5. Benedict Anderson, *Imagined Communities: Reflections on the Origin and Spread of Nationalism* (London: Verso, 1983).

6. Anderson, *Imagined Communities,* 6.

7. Manuel Castells, *The Information Age: Economy, Society, and Culture*, vol. 2, *The Power of Identity* (London: Blackwell, 1997), 29.

8. Joseph Lockard, "Progressive Politics, Electronic Individualism, and the Myth of the Virtual Community," in *Internet Culture,* ed. David Porter (New York and London: Routledge, 1997), 229. See also Ann Travers, *Writing the Public in Cyberspace: Redefining Inclusion on the Net* (London and New York: Garland Publishing, 2000).

9. Guy Debord, as cited in Howard Rheingold, *The Virtual Community: Homesteading on the Electronic Frontier* (Addison-Wesley, 1993), 298.

10. Jean Baudrillard, as cited in Derek Foster, "Community and Identity in the Electronic Village," in *Internet Culture,* 31.

11. Rheingold, *The Virtual Community*, 3.

12. Rheingold, *The Virtual Community*, 10.

13. Rheingold, *The Virtual Community*, 24. For a further discussion of new public spaces see Ray Oldenburg, *The Great Good Place: Cafes, Coffee Shops, Community Centers, Beauty Parlors, General Stores, Hangouts and How They Get You Through the Day* (New York: Paragon, 1991).

14. Robert Wright, "Hyper-Democracy," *Time*, 23 January 1995, 15.

15. Jonathan Gill, quoted in Craig McLaughlin, "Virtual Democracy," *San Francisco Bay Guardian*, 14 June 1995, 30.

16. Shawn Wilbur, "An Archaeology of Cyberspaces: Virtuality, Community, Identity," in *Internet Culture*, 14.

17. Dave Healy, "Cyberspace and Place: The Internet as Middle Landscape on the Electronic Frontier," in *Internet Culture*, 63. See also Michael Margolis and David Resnick, *Politics as Usual: The Cyberspace "Revolution"* (Thousand Oaks, Calif.: Sage, 2000).

18. Jeremy Rifkin, *The Age of Access: The New Culture of Hypercapitalism, Where All of Life Is a Paid-For Experience* (New York: Putnam, 2000), 108.

19. Rifkin, *The Age of Access*, 139.

20. James Madison, "Letter to Edmund Randolph (31 May 1789)," in *The Writings of James Madison*, vol. 5, ed. Gaillard Hunt (New York: Doubleday, Page & Co., 1904), 377.

21. Jürgen Habermas, *The Structural Transformation of the Public Sphere*, trans. Thomas Berger with Frederick Lawrence (Cambridge, Mass.: MIT Press, 1989). First published in 1962.

22. Habermas, *The Structural Transformation of the Public Sphere*, 282.

23. For a summary of these views, see Douglas Kellner, *Television and the Crisis of Democracy* (Boulder, Colo., and San Francisco: Westview, 1990); James Fishkin, *The Voice of the People: Public Opinion and Democracy* (New Haven, Conn.: Yale University Press, 1996); James Fallows, *Breaking the News: How the Media Undermine Democracy* (New York: Pantheon, 1996).

24. John Thompson, *Ideology and Modern Culture: Critical Social Theory in the Era of Mass Communication* (Stanford, Calif.: Stanford University Press, 1990).

25. James Jefferson Hunter, *Before the Shooting Starts: Searching for Democracy in America's Culture War* (New York: The Free Press, 1994), 98.

26. Patricia Aufderheide, "The Big Grab," *In These Times* 19, no. 15 (12 June 1995), 8–9.

27. Mark Poster, "Cyberdemocracy: The Internet and the Public Sphere," in *Internet Culture*, 205.

28. Allucquère Rosanne Stone, "Will the Real Body Please Stand Up? Boundary Stories About Virtual Cultures," in *Cyberspace: First Steps*, ed. Michael Benedikt (Cambridge, Mass.: MIT Press, 1991), 99.

29. Alexis de Tocqueville, *Democracy in America* (New York: A. A. Knopf, 1945); Lani Guinier, *The Tyranny of the Majority: Fundamental Fairness in Representative Democracy* (New York: Free Press, 1994).

30. John Dewey, *Democracy and Education: An Introduction to the Philosophy of Education* (New York: Macmillan, 1944); John Rawls, *A Theory of Justice* (Cambridge: Harvard University Press, 1971).

31. John Locke, *The Second Treatise of Civil Government* (Buffalo, N.Y.: Prometheus Books, 1986), 413.

32. Michael Walzer, "The Civil Society Argument," in *Dimensions of Radical Democracy,* ed. Chantal Mouffe (London and New York: Verso, 1991), 89–107; Paul Hirst, "Associational Democracy," in *Prospects for Democracy: North/South/East/ West,* ed. David Held (Stanford, Calif.: Stanford University Press, 1993), 112–135.

33. Amitai Etzioni, *Capital Corruption: The New Attack on American Democracy* (New Brunswick: Transaction Books, 1988); Amitai Etzioni, *The Spirit of Community: Rights, Responsibilities, and the Communitarian Agenda* (New York: Crown Books, 1993).

34. See, for example Robert Dahl, *A Preface to Economic Democracy* (Berkeley: University of California, 1984); David Held, *Models of Democracy* (Stanford, Calif.: Stanford University Press, 1987).

35. John Dunn, ed., *The Economic Limits of Modern Politics* (Cambridge: Cambridge University Press, 1990); Samuel Bowles and Herbert Gintis, *Democracy and Capitalism: Property, Community, and the Contradictions of Modern Social Thought* (New York: Basic Books, 1986).

36. Norberto Bobbio, *Which Socialism? Marxism, Socialism, and Democracy*, trans. Roger Griffin (London: Polity Press, 1987), 24. See also Norberto Bobbio, *The Future of Democracy: A Defense of the Rules of the Game,* trans. Roger Griffin (London: Polity Press, 1987).

37. Chantal Mouffe, "Democratic Politics Today," in *Dimensions of Radical Democracy,* ed. Chantal Mouffe (London and New York: Verso, 1991).

38. Ernesto Laclau and Chantal Mouffe, *Hegemony and Socialist Strategy* (London: Verso, 1985), 122.

39. Laclau and Mouffe, *Hegemony and Socialist Strategy.*

40. The recurrent accusation that radical democracy constitutes a linguistic argument with little material consequences emerged in a well-known exchange of articles in *New Left Review.* See Norman Geras, "Post-Marxism?" *New Left Review,* May/June 1987, 10–72; Ernesto Laclau and Chantal Mouffe, "Post-Marxism without Apologies," *New Left Review,* November/December 1987, 79–107; Norman Geras, "Ex-Marxism Without Substance: Being a Real Reply to Laclau and Mouffe," *New Left Review,* May/June 1988, 34–61.

41. Noam Chomsky, "Democracy's Slow Death," *In These Times,* 28 November-11 December 1994, 25.

42. Ziauddin Sardar and Jerome R. Ravetz, *Cyberfutures: Culture and Politics on the Information Superhighway* (New York: NYU Press, 1996).

43. Sardar and Ravetz, *Cyberfutures,* 15.

44. Sardar and Ravetz, *Cyberfutures,* 17.

45. Sardar and Ravetz, *Cyberfutures,* 18.

46. Sardar and Ravetz, *Cyberfutures,* 18.

47. Sardar and Ravetz, *Cyberfutures,* 19.

48. Sardar and Ravetz, *Cyberfutures,* 29.

49. Castells, *The Information Age,* 311–12.

50. Castells, *The Information Age,* 309.

51. Jean Maria Guehenno, as cited in Castells, *The Information Age,* 310.

52. Gary Chapman, "Tired Wired," *San Francisco Examiner,* 4 January 1994, D4. See also Paul Keegan, "The Digerati," *New York Times Magazine,* 21 May 1995, 38–46.

53. Chapman, "Tired Wired," D4.

54. Vivian Sobchack, "Democratic Franchise and the Electronic Frontier," in Sardar and Ravetz, *Cyberfutures,* 80.

55. Lockard, "Progressive Politics, Electronic Individualism, and the Myth of the Virtual Community," 227.

56. Lockard, "Progressive Politics, Electronic Individualism, and the Myth of the Virtual Community," 227.

57. Maria Fernandez, "Postcolonial Media Theory," *Third Text,* Summer 1999, 12. See also Beth Kolko, Lisa Nakamura, and Gilbert Rodman, eds., *Race in Cyberspace* (London and New York: Routledge, 2000).

58. Mark Poster, "Cyberdemocracy: The Internet and the Public Sphere," in *Internet Culture,* 203. See also Stephanie Gibson and Ollie Oviedo, eds., *The Emerging Cyberculture: Literacy, Paradigm, and Paradox* (Cresskill, N.J.: Hampton Press, 2000); Michael Margolis and David Resnick, *Politics as Usual: The Cyberspace "Revolution"* (Thousand Oaks, Calif.: Sage, 2000).

59. Gilles Deleuze and Felix Guattari, *A Thousand Plateaus: Capitalism and Schizo-phrenia* (Minneapolis: University of Minnesota, 1988), 360.

6

Reading Cyberculture

CURRENT CONTROVERSIES over the role of digital media in contemporary life have their roots in unresolved contradictions in the history of technology itself. As an area of study, technology largely was ignored through much of Western history. In the aristocratic culture of ancient Greece, the most revered forms of thinking addressed social, political, and theoretical concerns rather than what were considered the everyday banalities of technology.[1] Not unlike contemporary attitudes toward "technical schools" and "technicians," the idea of technology carried a crudely instrumental connotation. The conceptualization of "technology" in today's inclusive and comprehensive understanding of the term did not gain popular currency until after World War I. As the Western enlightenment was unfolding in the 1700s, technical ideas were considered endeavors in what were called the "mechanical arts" (material, practical, industrial), as opposed to the "fine arts" (ideal, creative, intellectual). As Leo Marx writes, "The habit of separating the practical and the fine arts served to ratify a set of overlapping invidious distinctions between things and ideas, the physical and the mental, the mundane and the ideal, female and male, making and thinking, the work of enslaved and free men"[2] This is not to suggest a negative view of technology—simply a resolutely practical one.

With the development of the biological and social sciences in the eighteenth and nineteenth centuries, technology came to be viewed as a natural manifestation of the human will to grow and prosper. This idea of technology as an organic and unremittingly positive "extension of man" provided the basis for what has been termed "technological instrumentalism." Within this commonsense framework, technology is viewed as a neutral tool that serves as an agent of social progress. Technological instrumentalism flourished in the nineteenth century with the development of such devices as the steam engine, locomotive, water mill, cotton gin, power loom, telegraph, and numerous other inventions that expanded human capacity and industrial productivity. Ruminating over these innovations in his famous "Sign of the Times" essay of 1829, Thomas Carlisle termed the coming era the "Age of Machinery."[3] But the technological revolution had other consequences as well. With the broad-based mechanization of the workplace, the character of labor began to change, as goods once made by hand were produced on the assembly line. As shoemakers, blacksmiths, and similar craftspeople were displaced by workers who operated machinery and punched a time clock, trades of many types became drained of their "artistic" elements. Attitudes toward work and leisure began to shift as a result. To a large extent creative activity ceased to be a part of one's workplace activity, but instead was redefined as something experienced off the clock.

Paralleling this mechanization of the individual's experience of work was the development of large-scale integrated "technological systems" to make such mechanization possible. Between 1870 and 1920 in the United States, enormous growth occurred in the development of electric power and light companies, telegraph and telephone systems, the chemical industry, transportation systems, and large-scale manufacturing. The mass production and distribution of a commodity like an automobile called into existence a complex constellation of variously skilled workers, suppliers, subcontractors, managers, supervisors, clerks, transporters, dealers, and service people. Railroad systems developed networks of tracks, equipment, conductors, communication networks, and ticket agents. Power grids were created as highways and housing developments sprang up across the nation.

Complementing this thoroughly modern evolution in material goods were similarly scientific methods of management. In this era the doctrines of Taylorism and Fordism emerged to enhance worker efficiency and workplace productivity, as employees came to be seen more as components of the larger technological system than as individuals. As labor became fragmented and systemized, new regimes of rationality, efficiency, and order emerged in the edifice of impersonal bureaucracies and hierarchical administrative structures. In an atmosphere of economic growth driven by the imperatives of the modern corporation, the ethos of the day was continual acceleration and accumulation. Over time, technology became invested with "a host of metaphysical properties and potencies, thus making it seem a determinate entity, a disembodied, autonomous, causal agent of social change—of history."[4] The legacy of these early technological systems and their ideological underpinnings of technological instrumentalism are still with us today, manifest in the burgeoning bioscience and information technology sectors that the popular media tell us are fueling the nation's economic recovery.

It is important to acknowledge the range of counterarguments that have arisen throughout the modern era—and especially during the post-World War II years—to question, contradict, and negate the unproblematized premises of such utopian visions of technological progress. Historian Andrew Feenberg has used the term *technological substantivism* to describe various strains of opposition to the overriding discourse of technological instrumentalism.[5] Substantive analyses do not see technology as neutral, but instead view it as the embodiment of social values. An early skeptic of instrumentalism, Martin Heidegger wrote that technology invariable creates relationships of control from which people struggle in vain to free themselves. As a substance existing throughout human history, the hidden secret of technology as a controlling force became manifest in the modern era. "It is impossible," Heidegger wrote, "for man to imagine a position outside of technology."[6]

Jacques Ellul, among other substantive critics, further elaborated on the distinct relationship of technology to modern society. To Ellul "technology has become autonomous" in its ability to structure human actions and relationships. Ellul was responding specifically to the way technological systems of the early twentieth century became transformed into "technocracies"—or technological bureaucracies—in which technology evolves into a branch of politics.[7] Within the autonomous logic of the technocracy, the original scientific impetus to develop systems for the Enlightenment goal of a better and more egalitarian society became subverted by the solipsistic imperatives of technology itself. Ellul's technocracies are self-replicating systems in which every action is rationalized as a contribution to technological improvement and expansion. As such they constitute one of the primary means by which the Weberian iron cage of bureaucracy becomes actualized.

These generalized notions of technological substantivism assumed a degree of heightened potency and specificity in the years following World War II. With Hiroshima, the nuclear arms race, and the U.S. involvement in the Vietnam War, public anxieties began to erode the unquestioned role of technology as instrument of social good. As myriad technologically based domestic products like television were introduced into the home, other voices were beginning to point out the environmental devastation created by unchecked industrial expansion. By the end of the 1960s the student movements of the New Left had given technocracy a name—the "military–industrial complex"—and were blaming it for a plethora of social ills ranging from ecological devastation to the corporate transformation of the university into the "multiversity." The activists sought a structural reorganization of technocracy to better serve the interests of democracy. Such sentiments deepened in the 1980s with the events of Chernobyl, Bhopal, the *Exxon Valdez;* growing recognition of the phenomena of acid rain, ozone depletion, and global warming; and the social devastation of Rust Belt communities brought on by the collapse of heavy industry.

Slowly the topic of technology began to emerge as an issue of intellectual concern in a variety of disciplines. In addition to critiques from the antiwar and environmental movements, important analyses of technology emerged from Marxist, feminist, and poststructuralist circles. The Marxist arguments addressed the overarching linkage of technology to markets. As discussed by Andrew Ross, early on technology was "dealt a hand in the power structure of capitalism (which is increasingly dependent on science-based industry), while its efficiency logic came to prevail over scientific management of everyday life."[8] The systematic effects of such social engineering have been widespread, from the reorganization of labor to the industrialization of culture and entertainment." This materialist critique differs from the substantive view of technology as a menace in its own right. Although lending itself easily to market exploitation, technology in this view was more a means than an end. As Ross concludes, "Capitalist reason, not technical reason, is still the order of the day."[9]

Feminist views of technology grew at first from critiques of science as a patriarchal system practiced by men and for men. Writers like Sandra Harding considered technology in epistemological terms, asking: Whose interests are served by a rationalist philosophy of science that posits the world in universal terms? According to whose logic are "objective" certainties of knowledge established? This feminist interrogation of objectivism soon gained currency in the social sciences, where the ethnocentric underpinnings of Western rationalism were further revealed. The answer to Harding's rhetorical question "Is Science Multicultural?" came back a resounding "no."[10] An important parallel to the feminist critique of objectivism emerged in analyses of language and representation. From such fundamental feminist issues as the critique of everyday speech emerged a more full-fledged inquiry into the role of linguistics in the development of thought and identity. Like objectivism, structuralist views of language posited a universal grammar in which rules and characteristics remain consistent from culture to culture. Also like objectivism, the structuralist view was too broad as a way of understanding the way meaning functions. The feminist critique of this singular worldview was soon adapted by visual theorists like Laura Mulvey and Teresa De Lauretis, who analyzed ways that media function as "technologies of gender."[11]

In the poststructuralist strain of this thinking, theorists questioned singular definitions of progress and rationality.[12] Michel Foucault in particular gained prominence in describing the "technologies of power" embedded in social institutions or such metaphorical constructs as the panopticon.[13] Although celebrated for their novelty, Foucault's views on technology can be seen as extensions of prior critiques of technocratic systems. For Foucault such systems create environments within which people are controlled, often unwittingly. Yet Foucault departs from earlier analyses in his acknowledgement of the partial or contingent role played by technology in the context of other influences. Perhaps the most significant element in Foucault's formulation lies in the allowances he makes for human agency to resist or subvert "regimes of domination" in productive terms.

The poststructuralist critique of science and technology also is significant in its eschewal of essentialism. Many early determinist and substantive views, as well as their critiques by Marxist and feminists, constructed technology as an unchanging phenomenon that carried the same characteristics across time and space. In viewing technology as a contingent entity that functions differently in various contexts, poststructuralism suggests that technology is not necessarily a linear and unstoppable force. This leaves open the possibility for a view of technology as progressive, hence yielding a critical space in which to engage its problems and potentials.

To Feenberg this dialectical view holds importance in its critical tolerance for rationality. Like it or not, rationalist objectivism holds a solid lock on the real-life discourses of science, jurisprudence, and education, to name but a few. As Feenberg writes,

> Whatever the ultimate status of scientific–technical knowledge, it is what we use for truth in making policy. We need far more specific arguments against technocracy that can play at that level. Furthermore, it is implausible to dismiss rationality as merely a Western myth and to flatten all distinctions which so obviously differentiate modern from premodern society. There is something special captured in notions such as modernization, rationalization, and reification.[14]

As we recognize the problems with universal claims of "truth," the need persists for provisional or local truths that can be used in communication. This implies that the task of making meaning will be more complex and labor intensive, but it also promises that differences will not be elided as a matter of course. All of these issues have assumed a greater complexity in recent years, with the introduction of accessible technology in the form of home computers and network interfaces. Formerly abstract ideas about the role of technology in everyday life have become a part of daily existence.

Cyberspace

As recently as a decade ago, no one would have predicted the ubiquitous role the Internet would play in society. The Internet was born in the 1970s as a military project to facilitate the exchange of technical data among weapons scientists. Called the Advanced Research Projects Agency Network (ARPANET), the original Net was conceived by the California-based RAND Corporation, a private think tank hired by the government to study issues of national security and public policy. Originally ARPANET was designed as a fail-safe communication system to be used in the event of nuclear war. The ARPANET system primarily remained the domain of academics until the 1980s, when personal computers and modems began to expand consumer access to this free service. The exponentially expanding market for equipment meant that before long, electronic bulletin boards and conferencing systems seemed to be springing up everywhere. In 1987 the Internet counted 10,000 hosts (organizers of electronic conversations); by 1992 the number had risen to 740,000. Today the number has reached the tens of millions.

So pervasive has the Internet become that it is difficult to overstate its role in the popular imaginary. The Internet is described in grand metaphors as a superhighway or mystical space with powers to restructure fundamental systems of communication, economic exchange, human consciousness, and civic policy. In comparison with other emergent digital media forms of the decade—the home computer, the CD-ROM, the interactive game—the development of networked systems has by far been the most pervasive innovation. Some compare the current era to the so-called Gutenberg Revolution that accompanied the development of the printing press. According to Internet promoters like Al Gore and Bill Gates, the networked personal computer has become a Rosetta stone to satisfy every variety of human want and need.

The era of cyberspace has been promoted endlessly in the mainstream electronic and print media, with specially dedicated "Internet hour" radio series, television news programs, and a regular progression of special issues of *Time, Newsweek,* and *U.S. News and World Report.* Magazines such as *Wired* and *Yahoo World* have enjoyed instant commercial success, and scholarly journals such as *Social Text, South Atlantic Quarterly,* and *Genders* have devoted special issues to the topic. And of course, there has been an endless outpouring of books with titles like *Being Digital, Internet Dreams, The Digital Dialectic,* and *Electronic Culture*—to name but a few.[15] All of this "talk" and "writing" about cyberspace has prompted more than one critic to observe how dependent this "new" digital medium is on the "old" communications media it is so often assumed to be replacing. In this way the "representation" of cyberspace plays an extremely important role in the ways it is understood. How we read, hear, and view the discourse of cyberspace both reflects and determines popular views of the topic. Although myriad taxonomies might be applied to the rapidly growing field of cyberculture, several broad categories of discourse seem to be emerging.

Cyberexceptionalism

The most common representation of cyberspace is that of a radically new medium born of the confluence of network technology and the rise of the personal computer. This position can be located within the instrumentalist school of thought described earlier as a distinctly modernist view of a technological progression in which one advance follows the next. Proponents of this view take great pains to argue that cyberspace offers an essential break—or paradigm shift—from past ways of artistic practice, communication, or social organization. Great emphasis is placed on the formal aspects of the medium: the ability of information technology to atomize or universalize data, its capacity to process large volumes of information at great speeds, or its ways of linking users across space and time.

In popular media and advertising the intent of such rhetoric is often relatively obvious, as technology manufacturers and resellers seek to promote the latest model of this or that product. This approach is nowhere more clearly demonstrated than in the words of Microsoft founder Bill Gates, who has amassed his personal fortune through development and sale of computer software. His book *Business@the Speed of Thought: Using a Digital Nervous System*, contains a twelve-step plan (with no apparent sense of self-irony) for corporate success tied completely to the use of computer networks.[16] Gates writes,

> If the 1980s were about quality and the 1990s were about re-engineering, then the 2000s will be about velocity. About how quickly business itself will be transacted. About how information access will alter the lifestyles of consumers and their expectation of business. . . . When the increase in velocity is fast enough, the very nature of business changes. To function in the new digital age, we have developed a new digital infrastructure. It's like the human nervous system.[17]

Borrowing liberally (and without attribution) from Marshall McLuhan, Gates outlines various methods of using e-mail to route customer complaints, communicate with managers, distribute online marketing reports, and set up "e-commerce" sales networks. In short, Gates grafts an assortment of relatively commonplace management practices to the Internet and asserts that the computer—not the attentive manager or skillful entrepreneur—is responsible for their effectiveness.

Of course Gates is hardly alone in this. The San Francisco-based *Wired* magazine has been promoting the concepts of the "netizen" (citizen of the Internet) and "digerati" (literati of the digital) models of information-age identity. Like the demographics for the magazine itself these identities invariably coalesce around values of young adulthood, upward mobility, and of course the latest technological toys. Packaged in a rhetoric of new-age libertarianism, the movement also projects an unmistakable message. As described by Michael Heim, "the 'digerati' celebrated by *Wired* magazine welcome the digital revolution and offer a central warning: you had better join or be crushed by the wheels of history."[18]

Former *Wired* staff writer Paulina Borsook explored the magazine and the culture it documents in her book *Cyberselfish: A Critical Romp Through the Terrible Libertarian Culture of High Tech.*[19] Founded in San Francisco in 1993, *Wired* initially sought to position itself as a high-tech *Rolling Stone* that was hip, smart, and dedicated to high journalistic standards. Over time the periodical's focus on the hyperbolic computer culture, coupled with *Wired's* own commercial success, allowed it to be swallowed by the cyberlibertarian ideology that defined Silicon Valley. By the mid-1990s *Wired* was regarded as the voice of the digerati class that worshipped technology, valorized corporate culture, and disdained government regulation. With a self-righteous contempt for anything outside of digital culture, *Wired's* pages rarely, if ever, featured material by or about women and minorities. And it never printed anything critical of technology or the corporate infrastructure of the computer industry.

Borsook divides technolibertarians philosophically into camps she calls "Ravers" and "Gilders," each with a symbolic patriarch. The Raver ideology of free-spirited antiestablishmentarianism is embodied in the persona of former Grateful Dead lyricist John Perry Barlow, famous for his Thoreaulike "Declaration of Independence in Cyberspace."[20] As Barlow wrote in an issue of *Spin,*

> Many federal governments are already both fibrillating with data-shock and increasingly incapable of convincing taxpayers who support them that they are getting anything like their money's worth. I think it's unlikely that there will be a federal government left on the planet in 50 years. . . . It's difficult to enforce a credible order upon people whose activities can take place in any terrestrial jurisdiction.[21]

Gilder ideology is more traditionally conservative in both social and economic terms, and is typified by the thinking of former Reagan speechwriter and antifeminist George Gilder, who, oddly enough, became a frequent contributor to *Wired*. Quick to bash the government, Gilder frequently celebrated the entrepreneurial impulse, as in this section from his book *The Spirit of Enterprise:*

> Bullheaded, defiant, tenacious, creative, entrepreneurs continued to solve the problems of the world even faster than the world could create them. The achievements of enterprise remained the highest testimony to the mysterious

strength of the human spirit. Confronting the perennial perils of human life . . . the entrepreneur finds a higher source of hope than reason, a deeper well of faith than science, a farther reach of charity than welfare.[22]

Driven by these two brands of libertarianism, *Wired*'s free-market techno-boosterism became its defining ethos. It also left room for little else. As gushing editorial content and glitzy advertising material increasingly seemed to mimic each other, the gaps and absences became more apparent by the end of the 1990s. *Wired* resolutely ignored such glaring issues as gender bias and age discrimination in the computer industry, the growing divide between information haves and have-nots, the greed and stinginess of the Silicon Valley corporate elite—in short, any of the material realities that contradicted its utopian view of cyberspace. In its place was a new brand of technological fetishism, the elevation of technology to the level of aesthetics and style. As described by R. L. Rutsky in *Wired,* high tech was "treated as having a value in itself. Thus endowed with imminent value, high tech tends to be seen less as a means or tool for human use than as something autonomous of human control."[23] The *Wired* program has been extremely influential. Now its thinking is reproduced in dozens of similar magazines, Web sites, and books that celebrate the digital age. Even a staid publication like the *New York Times* publishes a weekly computer lifestyle section titled "Circuits."

Within academic literature cyberexceptionalism takes the form of a giddy modernism, with intellectuals expounding on the novel implications of information technology. Most frequently one finds a celebration of the non-physicality of software and computer networks—the ways that computers alter our relationship to space and time. After all, this is the postindustrial age, the era following the days of heavy manufacturing, manual labor, and industrial pollution. In the 1980s, analysts spoke of an industrial economy giving way to a service economy. In the 1990s terms like *knowledge industries* and *information workers* entered the common vocabulary. Early in that decade, cyberspace boosters Mitch Kapor and Barlow—founders of the Electronic Frontier Foundation—wrote that "old concepts of property, expression, identity, movement, and contest, based as they are on physical manifestation, do not apply succinctly in a world where there can be none."[24]

One of the most comprehensive discussions of the new spatiality of the cyberworld appeared in William J. Mitchell's book *City of Bits: Space, Place, and the Infobahn.* Dean of architecture and planning at MIT, Mitchell asserts that a radical transformation is taking place in the way people understand both the imaginary spaces created online and the physical spaces they inhabit. The metaphors are telling. One has an e-mail "address" along an information "highway" that can lead you through a "domain" server to a

Web "site" or a chat "room"—not to mention the more literal dungeons, cities, or football fields created by computer games. As Mitchell writes, "The worldwide computer network—the electronic agora—subverts, displaces, and radically redefines our notions of gathering place, community, and urban life."[25] In redefining our relationship in virtual worlds, the computer is changing our relationships to the material world. As communication becomes faster and more pervasive, the necessity to physically travel to a library, bookstores, or stockbroker diminishes. As Mitchell puts it, "So, 'inhabitation' takes on a new meaning—one that has less to do with parking your bones in architecturally defined space and more with connecting your nervous system to nearby electronic organs. Your room and your home will become part of you, and you will become part of them."[26]

Another significant category of cyberexceptionalism involves vision or "representation" on the computer screen. Although proponents of these ideas usually assert an underlying postmodern character to computer "simulations" of reality, much of the actual discussion of the media has a distinctly modernist tenor. As Peter Lunenfeld writes in the introduction to his book *The Digital Dialectic,*

> No matter how much digital media resemble film or television, they are fundamentally different. The computer, when linked to network, is unique in the history of technological media: it is the first widely disseminated system that offers the user the opportunity to create, distribute, receive, and consume audio visual content with the same box. Thus, theorists have to strive to create new models of commentary that consider more than consumption or spectatorship.[27]

Similar sentiments are espoused by UC San Diego professor Lev Manovitch in his widely cited essay "What Is Digital Cinema?" For Manovitch digital technology has introduced a fundamentally new way of conceiving film and television narrative due to the pervasiveness of computer animation and special effects. No longer need discussions be limited to debates over the extent to which photographic technologies mediate a viewer's relationships to the real. In cyberspace, where entire fantasy worlds are more the norm than the exception, nothing is "real." As Manovitch writes, "Cinema's public image stressed the auras of 'reality' captured on film, thus implying that cinema was about photographing what existed before the camera, rather than about creating the 'never-was' of special effects."[28]

Significant in this formulation is the binary real/unreal, body/mind split that characterizes Enlightenment epistemology. This model was criticized in feminist, multiculturalist, and poststructuralist circles for the invariable preference it yields to mental position over the physical and the way it fails to acknowledge the constructed character of all representation and human consciousness. More to the point, this widespread privileging of the idealized aspects of the digital by cyberexceptionalists serves to either mystify or obscure social conditions in the noncyber world. Mitchell acknowledges the dangerous political implications of this Cartesian split. On one hand, the idealized world of the Internet creates a "new" space of wonderful opportunity. "Can we use the Infobahn as an equalizing mechanism—a device for providing enhanced access to these benefits for the geographically isolated, the home bound elderly, the sick and disabled, and those who cannot afford wheels?" Mitchell asks.[29] Indeed, the ability of the Internet to connect remote locations to the new decentralized "space" virtual society offers would seem to offer utopian possibilities. But outside this idealized space, broader socioeconomic systems remain unchanged—including those that undergird high technology itself. Mitchell writes that for all of the positive rhetoric,

> At the same time, there are vigorous *centralizing* forces at work. Production processes remain ultimately dependent on appropriation and transformation of matter, so industrial locations are still largely determined by local availability (Silicon Valley centralization of capital) of raw materials and access to labor markets. Furthermore, the initial development of an advanced telecommunications infrastructure is likely to favor existing urban centers (with their high and profitable concentrations of information work) over small towns and remote areas.[30]

As in the broader analyses of technological systems, specific critiques have been made of cybermodernist utopianism from materialist and identity-based perspectives. From the materialist or Marxist side come views like that of Mitchell, which focus on the ways that business interests promote and benefit from the current digital mania. Books like *Resisting the Virtual Life* by James Brook and Ian Boal, *The Age of Missing Information* by Bill McKibben, *Cyberspace Divide* by Brian Loader, *The Politics of Cyberspace* by Chris Toulouse and Timothy W. Luke, and *Virtual Realities and Their Discontents* by Robert Markley share a common view that large multinational corporations and a profit-driven U.S. stock market have created a voracious high-technology industry that is widening the gap between rich and poor people, as well as rich and poor nations.[31] In a set of arguments reminiscent of Ben Bagdikian's treatise on the communications industry, *The Media Monopoly*, these writers warn of the dangers when a relatively small number of powerful corporations can commandeer a large percentage of such dynamic industry.[32] Related to these generalized concerns over the ambitions of cybercapitalism are more specific issues involving access to technology, copyright and intellectual property, online privacy, and e-commerce.

The more extreme of these critiques question, not only the instrumental expansion of cyberspace by self-interested entrepreneurs, but also the very character of this new medium on substantive terms. In his best-selling book *Silicon Snake Oil: Second Thoughts on the Information Highway,* Clifford Stoll states that computer networks "isolate us from one another and cheapen the meaning of actual experience. They work against literacy and creativity. They will undercut our schools and libraries."[33] To Stoll and others, the Internet is so seductive that it encourages overuse and even addiction. As Stoll writes,

> It's an unreal universe, a soluble tissue of nothingness. While the Internet beckons brightly, seductively flashing an icon of knowledge-as-power, this non-place lures us to surrender our time on earth. A poor substitute it is, the virtual reality where frustration is legion and where—in the holy names Education and Progress—important aspects of human interactions are relentlessly devalued.[34]

Feminist critiques began with complaints about the exclusion of women and girls from the patriarchal culture of the technology and computers. Books like Roberta Furger's *Does Jane Compute? Preserving Our Daughters' Place in the Cyber Revolution* brought to light the way boys are steered toward computers and girls away from them by childrearing practices, the popular media, the toy and game industry, schools, and clubs, as well as computer and software makers.[35] But the story does not end there. As the computer and Internet have become ubiquitous elements of everyday life, and as companies have woken up to the fact that they were ignoring a huge market segment, more and more computer products are designed with women in mind.

In more academic circles, scholars like Anne Balsamo, Margaret Morse, Constance Penley, Sadie Plant, Sandy Stone, and Sherry Turkle have been addressing the complex and often contradictory relationships women have with computer technology. Turkle's *Life on the Screen* takes up the way network environments permit the transformation or masking of identity. Balsamo's *Technologies of the Gendered Body* discusses how computers, imaging systems, and cosmetic technologies like plastic surgery enable bodily manipulations for better or worse.[36] Certainly the most widely cited feminist thinker on these issues is Donna Haraway, whose formulation of the machine/human synthesis in her 1985 "Cyborg Manifesto" offered a positive view of technology and female subjectivity.[37] Like other feminists writing about imaging technologies and entertainment media, Haraway was hardly sanguine about the negative implications of digital vision or what I have been calling cybermodernism:

> The eyes have been used to signify a perverse capacity—honed to perfection in the history of science tied to militarism, capitalism, colonialism, and male

supremacy—to distance the knowing subject from everybody and everything in the interest of unfettered power. The instruments of visualization in multinationalist, postmodernist culture have compounded these meanings of disembodiment. The visualizing technologies are without apparent limit; the eye of the ordinary primate like us can be endlessly enhanced by sonographic systems, magnetic resonance imaging, artificial intelligence-linked graphics manipulation systems, scanning electron microscopes, computer-aided tomography scanners, color-enhancement techniques, satellite surveillance systems, home and office VDTs, cameras for every purpose from filming mucous membrane lining the gut cavity of a marine worm living in the vent gases on a fault line between continental plates to mapping a planetary hemisphere elsewhere in the solar system.[38]

Much of the idealized discourse of cyberspace discounts such materialist exigencies, but it does something else as well. Paul Virilio has explained how formulations of "cyberspace," the "Infobahn," and the like seem to encourage thinking that minimizes or smoothes over issues of difference: "The negative aspect of these information superhighways is precisely this loss of orientation regarding alterity, this disturbance in the relationship with the other."[39] Needed are conversations about technology that address these absences, erasures, or confusions. Indeed it is in writing that addresses difference and identity that some of the most powerful analysis of technology is emerging. Certainly the psychoanalytic and Foucauldian-inspired writing of Haraway and other feminist theorists addresses gendered technologies of power and control, and thus begins to tackle the ways that science has been used in very real ways to sexualize and regulate the body. Whether one is discussing fad diets, prosthetic limbs, HIV research, or the general exclusion of women from network "communities," this focus on social technologies and physical regulation anchors futuristic speculation in the lived experience of human subjects.

In this light it is important to remember that little more than a decade ago access to cyberspace required membership in an elite community: the university. Now one needs access to a computer, modem, phone line, and Internet provider—criteria that still exclude poor people and certain communities of color in disproportionate numbers. As argued by Joseph Lockard, cyberspace itself is unmistakably signed with Euro-American Whiteness.

Race and ethnicity are simply not up for discussion in cyberspace social theory, and their very absence identifies unsubstantiated presumptions of community. The featurelessness of a presumptive non-racial ethnicity in cyberspace fails to correspond with the real and diverse communities around us. Even as ethnic/racial user groups establish themselves on the Internet, they disappear from public view, accessed only by those interested. Non-physicality elides their presence and alterity.[40]

Placed in a more global context, the very experience of networked communication, of digital aesthetics, reproduces a Western, specifically Cartesian, spatial model of representation, not unlike that of the cinema, creating a viewing subject occupying a privileged vantage point that is apart from the world viewed, and that permits that world to be constructed as something to be examined, manipulated, or owned. As Cameron Bailey explains, this creates a "self/other representational model that constructs a center/margin epistemology privileging the cybersubject as male, white, straight, able bodied, and dominant classed."[41]

To get specific for a moment, one need only look to the insider language of the online world that excludes outsiders, not only with a technical jargon of *MUDs, MOOs, avatars,* and *spam.* This constitutes an interpretive community (in the sense described by Stanley Fish) predicated on a set of exclusionary rules and "netiquette" that is far from civil. In any visit to an online chat room one will observe voluminous anti-Semitic, racist, homophobic, and especially sexist speech, giving lie to the myth of a disembodied or colorless cyberspace. Does the Internet encourage such behavior from otherwise polite individuals or does it attract bigots? Regardless, the experience of Internet use among women, people of color, lesbian women, and gay men is to foreground their identities while erasing them. It is just this double bind that needs further attention so that digital aesthetics does not become synonymous with the Microsoft monopolization of identity itself.

Digital Postmodernists

Critique of cybermodernism's monolithic discourse of rationality and progress attaches itself to the postmodern, poststructuralist, and deconstructionist movements that have influenced the Western world so profoundly for the past three decades. The epistemological paradox of all such "post" movements derives from their claims of separation from the schools of thought they assail, and produces two important questions. First, does an idea like postmodernism, which questions all modernist assumptions, constitute a distinctly different movement, or is it simply an extension and replication of modernism's underlying structure? Second, does an idea like postcolonialism imply the end of the colonial era, or simply a more contemporary way of addressing it? I pose these questions as a form of caveat for the "post" approaches to cyberspace that follow, especially since several of them have been challenged as ineffective or mistaken critiques of modernist ideology.

During the late 1990s a small explosion erupted in the world of academic writing on digital technology, as numerous scholars recognized the resemblance between computer networks and various postmodern theories of knowledge. Far from a modest critique of modernism, these writers latched onto the notion that the Internet—specifically its form of writing known as hypertext—constituted a long-sought physical embodiment of several abstract ideas. One of the central figures in this discussion is George P. Landow and his book *Hypertext: The Convergence of Contemporary Critical Theory and Technology*.[42] Landow writes that through this "convergence" "we must abandon conceptual systems founded upon center, margin, hierarchy, and linearity and replace them with ones of multilinearity, nodes, links, and networks." Along with works like Richard A. Lanham's *The Electronic Word*, Landow lays out this fundamental premise with tedious literality.[43] As Landow writes in his introduction,

> The many parallels between computer hypertext and critical theory have many points of interest, the most important of which, perhaps, lies in the fact that critical theory promises to theorize hypertext and hypertext promises to embody and thereby test aspects of theory, particularly those concerning textuality, narrative, and the roles or functions of reader and writer. Using hypertext, critical theorists will have, or now already have, a new laboratory.[44]

It is telling that the early proclamations of these ideas emerged from language professors like Lanham, whose theoretical discourse has been criticized as being so bound up in the abstraction that it has lost relevance to the "material" world. Such thinking openly acknowledges its debt to theorists like Roland Barthes and Jacques Derrida, both of whom explored the difficulties words have in communicating ideas. The fundamental semiotics practiced by these theorists early in their careers seemed especially relevant in its distillation of communication into tiny interchangeable pieces of meaning resembling "bits" of computer language. As Landow writes, "digitization is desubstantiating the entire world of arts and sciences. This common denominator of the arts and letters forces upon us a rhetoric of the art like none seen before."[45] Beyond this, Barthes' notions of the "text" as a collaborative event between reader and writer lent itself especially to the workings of the Internet, where e-mail and chat rooms create the illusion of a visible space between people made of words. Derrida's critiques of written sequentiality and writerly authority similarly were recognized easily in the Internet's tendency to fragment communication and level the ground among speakers.

Such thinking soon ran beyond the linguistics classroom, as scholars across the humanities, arts, and silences picked up the ball. Sociologist Sherry Turkle echoed the desire to see theory given a body, asserting that during "the past decade, the mechanical engines of computers have been grounding the radically nonmechanical philosophy of postmodernism."[46] Taking matters a step further, Turkle opines,

> Computer technology not only "fulfills the postmodern aesthetic" as Lanham would have it, heightening and concretizing the postmodern experience, but helps that aesthetic hit the street as well as the seminar room. Computers embody postmodern theory and bring it down to earth.[47]

Other strains of cyberpostmodern inspiration derive from theorists of vision and communication. Here Jean Baudrillard became a favorite both for his early formulation of the simulacrum and his later writing addressing computer technology. Baudrillard's infamous assertion of the primacy of representations over their referents, the replacement of things with images, again matched the experience of people who spent long hours staring at televisions or computer screens. In a televisual world it seemed entirely possible that the need for "authentic" or "real" experience would eventually disappear—as in the worlds of MUDs, MOOs, and other online "spaces" inhabited by fictional personals, avatars, or "intelligent agents." In this sense cyberpostmodernists link the modernist notion of a technical innovation to an altered representational scheme.

In an approach reminiscent of communication theorists like Marshall McLuhan and Neil Postman, historian Mark Poster gave shape to these ideas by stressing the importance of the medium in which ideas are conveyed. In *The Mode of Information*, Poster presented a three-part model of communication.[48] Stages one and two, oral and written communication, have contributed to the current third stage of electronic communication that is unique, according to Poster, in the psychic distance it permits. Unlike face-to-face talk or autonomously authored writing, electronic discourse allows a disembodied and unstable communication. Significant in Poster's formulation is his reluctance to say, as many others have said, that postmodern theory is *the same as* digital experience. There is simply a resemblance on a certain level.

Of course, more is at stake than the form through which ideas are exchanged, for the form influences the way people think and feel as they communicate. It alters their experience as subjects. All the theorists discussed in this section assert to varying degrees that language and media play an important role in how we understand who we are, what we know, and how we exchange information. When this powerful set of theoretical ideas is mixed with the ideology of technological promise, a catalyzing effect occurs. The optimism characteristic of this digital postmodernism is typified in an essay by Anna Sampaio and Janni Aragon, titled "To Boldly Go (Where No Man Has Gone Before): Women and Politics in Cyberspace."[49] These authors make the theoretical link between subjectivity and power, arguing that the Internet levels the playing field among electronic participants in electronic conversations. By stripping communication of consistent attribution (by allowing people to mask their identities) the Net encourages subversion, especially by women. As Sampaio and Aragon put it, "New informational technologies threaten the prominence of the autonomous rational masculinized subject as well as the existence of traditional hierarchies inscribed within print and spoken language systems."[50] In doing so they "allow for alternative language systems to emerge and for these languages to construct alternate subjectivities, as well as the implications these new subjects bring for a different type of feminist politics."[51]

Other writers take a somewhat less overdetermined view of cyberspace. Film theorist Bill Nichols draws a distinction between the cold artificiality of digitally mediated experience and the romantic aura of authentic objects that Walter Benjamin discussed at such great length. Significantly, Nichols begins to address the tendency of cyberenthusiasts to romanticize the characteristics of the medium. In a work titled "The Work of Culture in the Age of Cybernetic Systems," Nichols writes,

> The chip is pure surface, pure simulation of thought. Its material surface is its meaning without history, without depth, without aura, affect, or feeling. The copy reproduces the world, the chip simulates it. It is the difference between being able to remake the world and being able to efface it. The micro-electronic chip draws us into a realm, a design for living, that fosters a fetishized relationship with the simulation as a new reality all its own based on the capacity to control, within the domain of simulation, what had once eluded control beyond it. The orchids of immediate reality that Benjamin was wont to admire have become the paper flowers of cybernetic simulation.[52]

Nichols suggests that there may be something more taking place than the simple transformation of experience by technology. His evocation of Benjamin is significant, since the contemporary history of art and the marketing of art photography fundamentally disproved his premise that reproducibility would rob original objects of their ritual value. History has demonstrated that although media can play a significant role in the way ideas are communicated, it is a partial role and nothing more.

More strident critics of the convergence of critical theory and cybertechnology assert that a fundamental misunderstanding of deconstruction lies behind this utopian enthusiasm. For theorists like Barthes and Derrida, the "text" is first a metaphysical concept pertaining to the general function of language. Naming it as a particular form of communication—like a spoken "text," a printed textbook, or a computer-mediated hypertext—misses the point. The "work" is mistaken as the "text." As stated by Richard Grusin, the "force of the Derridian critique is to demonstrate the way in which thought and speech are always already a form of writing. Deconstruction does not need to be instantiated or embodied in new electronic technologies; for Derrida, writing is always a technology and always electronic."[53] This misapplication of deconstructionist premises has implications beyond the mere narrowing of a general principle to a specific application. It robs the theory of its subversive capacity to destabilize the way meaning is generated on many levels. It also appropriates and thereby confuses some of deconstruction's most potent political capacities.

To argue that hypertext by itself decenters the subject and destabilizes its authority is to invest in a medium the capacity to determine the way people send and receive information. It overlooks the fundamental insight of poststructuralism that nothing exerts such an absolute power, whether utopian or otherwise. From early proponents of reception theory in media to more subtle Foucauldian formulations of capillary power, premises of indeterminacy, partiality, and reciprocity have been formulated as aspects of the way people think, not the tools they use. As Grusin puts it, "The discursive logic of electronic authorship seems almost invariably to marginalize or elide its own central insights, either by making the technology itself transparent or by eliding the complicated discursive relationships between power and knowledge."[54]

On one level this might seem like a simple issue of intellectual hair splitting. After all, what does it matter how a bunch of college professors think of their computers? Without overstating the limited social role that intellectuals and teachers play, these individuals constitute some of the few voices in digital discourse that might question the overriding boosterism of corporate CEOs, politicians, journalists, and most important, young people. Lost in much of the contemporary discourse of cyberspace is the extent to which it functions as a prime mode of communication, diversion, skill-building—in short, education—for kids of all ages, almost all of whom lack the critical tools to engage the medium. When intellectuals are calling a highly commodified medium of advertising, pay-for-access, and actual sales an instrument of educational innovation, there is a serious lapse occurring. Some writers go as far as to suggest a radical pedagogical potential in a medium that purportedly inverts teacher/student hierarchies and empowers the disempowered in a classroom. Clearly this is investing a great deal in a technology. On a more general political level the problems are similar, as writer after writer asserts the revolutionary capacity of computers to undermine power and promote egalitarianism. Lanham in particular claims that "the electronic word democratizes the world of arts and letters," stating that "the people who developed the personal computer considered it a device of radical democratization from its inception."[55]

Less typical of cyberpostmodernists are those who take a critical stand, asserting the decentered subjectivity produced by the Internet exerts a destabilizing and mystifying influence. In *The Age of Access*, Jeremy Rifkin argues that as more and more of experience has been rendered digitally and circulated on the Internet, people have lost touch with authentic experience and human relationships. This results in a form of alienation that ultimately results in a degradation of community and failure of politics. As he writes, "The fast pace of a hyper-real, nanosecond culture shortens the individual and collective temporal horizon to the immediate moment."[56] Rifkin adds that "there is no great concern with making history but only making up interesting stories to live by."[57] Like some of the exceptionalists discussed earlier, Rifkin sees a profound paradigm shift evoked in digital culture that is probably irreversible. But to his credit, Rifkin moves beyond what seems to be a totalizing view of cyberspace in urging legal action and government regulation of the medium.

Some of the most systematic critiques of such cyberpostmodernist reveling were anthologized by Markley in *Virtual Realities and Their Discontents*. In Markley's analysis, cyberspace is not so much a "new" idea as it is a repository for a variety of conventional ideologies disguised as novelty: "Cyberspace is a consensual cliche, a dumping ground for repackaged philosophies about space, subjectivity, and culture: it does not offer a breakthrough in human, cyborgian, evolution, but merely (though admittedly) a seductive means to reinscribe fundamental tensions within Western concepts of identity and reality."[58] To Markley it is precisely the familiarity of conventional formulations of class, gender, race, and technology that have made cyberspace so acceptable to so many people. In this way cyberspace becomes yet another cultural form in which its representation (how it is perceived or thought about) can be viewed as a site of political contestation. Markley adds, "Technology never escapes politics. The fiction of cyberspace is useful precisely to the extent that it allows its proponents to imagine an androcentric reality in which threatening, messy, or recalcitrant (and invariably feminized) nature never intrudes."[59]

Cowboys, Communitarians, and Poets

The consensual cliché of cyberspace has generated a plethora of metaphors, proffering the digital world as a mythic frontier, an idealized community, and the means of poetic return to origins. Certainly it takes little imagination to recognize the parallels between the unexplored territory of the cyberworld and the "new world" imagined by the colonizers of the modern world. This ethos of exploration, discovery, and conquest becomes manifest most explicitly in entities with names like the Electronic Frontier Foundation (EFF), an early Internet nonprofit organization dedicated to preserving "freedom" of expression online. In some ways this masculinized formulation of the Internet as colonial battleground can be seen as an extension of historic patterns of Enlightenment advance, a compulsive search for expansion and progress. In instances where the historic frontier is not evoked, one finds an allegorical substitute. As Fredric Jameson has pointed out, the "fiction" of science fiction is often simply a reworked version of past history projected onto the screen of a purportedly distant future.[60] Certainly the cyberpunk novels that first emerged in the 1980s by writers like William Gibson and Bruce Sterling featured solitary male heroes struggling with a lawless society in a new world.[61] For the most part computer games even more crudely place the typically male game player in the role of a combatant in an often highly sexualized drama in games such as *Blade Runner* and *Doom*. Other games like the well-known *Tomb Raider* series may feature female protagonists, but do so in highly objectified and sexualized terms. The prime motive of these books and games in what Andrew Ross terms "a baroque edifice of adolescent male fantasies" is a desire for dominance and control.[62] But it is important to realize that such a compulsive desire can never be satisfied—and for that reason is continually remembered, repeated, and reconstituted. Writing of this imaginary landscape, Dave Healy states that "no frontier is final—only new for a while, then destabilized and contested, eventually transcended and absorbed into our collective pioneer spirit, our eternal restlessness, our longing for space and our attachment to place."[63]

The metaphor of the Old West takes another form in the highly influential writing of Howard Rheingold. In his book *The Virtual Community: Homesteading on the Electronic Frontier,* Rheingold applies a communitarian philosophy to the idea of the group conversation enabled by the Internet.[64] Chat rooms, electronic bulletin boards, list serves, newsgroups, and various multiuser environments create the sensation of a "group" brought together by a shared interest. According to Rheingold they also satisfy the very primary human instinct to forge communities in a very literal sense. Rheingold writes,

> There's always another mind there. It's like having the corner bar, complete with old buddies and delightful newcomers and new tools waiting to take home and fresh graffiti and letters, except instead of putting on my coat, shutting down the computer, and walking to the corner, I just download my telecom program and there they are. It's a place.[65]

It's a place that for Rheingold becomes an extension of nonvirtual experience: "Not only do I inhabit my virtual communities; to the degree that I carry around their conversations in my head and begin to mix it up with them in real life, my virtual communities also inhabit my life. I've been colonized."[66]

Here again one finds a remarkable investment in technology as a means of actualizing a range of discursive formations that purportedly reterritorialize the world. As David Porter writes in the introduction to his critical anthology *Internet Culture,* "virtual community is the illusion of community, where there are no real people and no real community. It is a term used by idealistic technophiles, who fail to understand that the authentic cannot be engendered through technology."[67] Although generally acknowledging that the Internet replicates existing relations of commerce and identity, these cheerleaders of the electric frontier like Rheingold, Mitch Kapor, John Perry Barlow, and Benjamin Woolley generally overlook the imperialistic, logocentric implications of this new space, as well as the extent to which life on the Web obfuscates the extent to which space in the "real" world continues to define who people are and what they can do.

If virtual communities do exist in any sense with genuine material consequences, it is as multinational corporations who use computer networks to manipulate labor markets, facilitate plant closures, enable just-in-time production, capitalize on currency fluctuations, subvert import/export regulations, and generally exploit less powerful populations around the globe. As discussed throughout this chapter, a persistent characteristic of digital discourse is the obfuscation of politics or the refusal to acknowledge them. Although lip service is sometimes paid to electoral politics via the "electronic town meeting" à la Ross Perot, the tendency of both popular and academic writers is to focus on cyberspace in an extremely romantic sense. Whether the goal is adventure or community, the overriding ethos evokes a traditional Platonic metaphysics in which ideal forms are privileged over material objects. For some writers this focus on the "poetry" of cyberspace is its essentialist rationale. Digital technology becomes the means of achieving the transcendent and unified subjectivity that has been the desire of Western philosophy for centuries. Jeffrey Fisher uses the term *technosophy* to designate this peculiar embodiment of humanistic desire.

> Technosophy encourages us to forget about social problems, specifically insofar as collective intelligence seems to require collective amnesia. Technosophy constructs cyberspace as a postmodern version of a medieval paradise, a space of transcendence in which evil and responsibility are left behind in a blissful conjunction with the really real.[68]

For some this utopian vision can be quite mystical. David Tomas asserts that computers will allow us "to overthrow the sensorial and organic architecture of the human body, this by disembodying and reformatting its sensorium in powerful, computer generated, digitized spaces."[69] Marcos Novak extends the hyperbole further, suggesting that "cyberspace is a completely spatialized visualization of all information in global information processing systems."[70]

The epistemologies of these ideas have historical roots in the sixteenth-century thinking of Rene Descartes and others who believed that the entire world could be understood through the "pure" language of mathematics. Such systems as math and optics demonstrated the existence of God and made it possible for humankind to access the divine natural order. Contemporary users adopt these ideas with varying degrees of skepticism. Benjamin Woolley sees a direct correspondence between the digital bit structure of cyberspace and the "mathematical structure of nature" and the fundamental "computability of the universe."[71] Like the hypertext utopianists discussed earlier, Woolley sees a means to concretize a philosophy via the Internet, this time in the manner of a formalism that would convert information into decontextualized formulas—seemingly without intention or agency. In a similar fashion, Michael Heim formulates his "erotic ontology of cyberspace" using the work of seventeenth-century thinker Gottlieb Leibnitz. Heim is attracted by Leibnitz's belief that all problems were soluble through a language of scientific objectivity. As Heim writes,

> The first step is to create a universal medium in which to communicate. With universal language, you can translate all human notions into the same basic set of symbols. Through a shared language, many discordant ways of thinking can exist under a single roof. Once disagreements in attitude or belief are translated into matching symbols, they can yield to logical operations. Problems that earlier seemed insoluble can stand on common ground.[72]

Like Woolley, Heim's epistemology posits an objective language that creates a wholly objective observer, detached from the material world by virtue of immersion in a virtual computer environment. By any estimate, this constitutes an instrumentalist position in its investment of neutrality and universality in a machine. But more than that, it represents a regression in its suggestion that the "real" world has no relationship with the "virtual" world. This widely held view among cyberenthusiasts holds a genuine danger in the way it reinforces a divide between ideal and material existence. As Markley puts it, "The fiction of cyberspace is useful precisely to the extent that it allows its proponents to imagine an androcentric reality in which threatening, messy, or recalcitrant (and invariable feminized) nature never intrudes."[73] This is the very problem at the heart of the "virtual class" that so greatly concerns Kroker, Weinstein, and others.

Much has been written about the solipsism that such binary thinking produces in enabling individuals to imagine a unified subjectivity. To Richard Coyne, the "technoromanticism" of a digital culture obsessed with cosmic "wholeness" or "unity" is simply a reaction against a world seemingly defined by scientific objectivity and certainty.[74] The result is a pathological interest in the romantic attributes of human feeling, emotion, and artistic expression. To Lacan the compulsive misrecognition of the self as whole is a symptom of desire or lack. It constitutes a means to alleviate an existential anxiety that can never be alleviated. In short, it is a delusional form of consciousness. Needed instead are models of subjectivity, models of cyberspace that do not split the world along subject/object or ideal/real dichotomies. Needed are ways of thinking about virtuality that either permit a dialogue among these realms or celebrate the possibilities of multiple identities. As Heim has recently written in his formulation of what he terms *virtual realism*,

> The challenge is not to end the oscillation between idealism and realism but to find the path that goes through them. It is not a synthesis in the Hegelian sense of a result achieved through logic. Neither is it a synthesis arising from the warfare of the two sides. Rather, virtual realism is an existential process of criticism, practice, and conscious communication.[75]

Clearly there is much work to be done in dismantling the unproductive dualisms that have characterized cyberculture in its early phases. As obvious as the binary logic of the computer may seem to some, is important to resist the tendency to reduce the conceptualization of cyberspace to zeros and ones. The popularity of this simplistic "digital" model is contributing to the vain self-satisfaction of the digerati and a nascent cyber-conservatism. Unchecked these attitudes will continue to reinforce traditional regimes of power and control in the guise of innovation and efficiency. Beneath the new-age hipness of *Wired* magazine lies an entrenched ideology of xenophobia and compulsive consumption. Beneath the kinder and gentler façade of a smiling Bill Gates lie the brutal competitiveness and legal chicanery of Microsoft.

Rather than regarding the binary structure of the information bit as a metaphor, perhaps cyberspace offers another model in the image of the distributed network. In *A Thousand Plateaus*, Gilles Deleuze and Felix Guattari evoke the "rhizome" to represent a structure of "connection and heterogeneity" that ruptures the mystification of binary forms.[76] It suggests multiple perspectives and levels of meaning, much like that of the Internet. But before one drifts down the path of hypertext utopianists, it is essential to point out

that such a model is simply a model—not a physical embodiment of principle. As Deleuze and Guattari put it, "A method of a rhizome type, on the
contrary, can analyze language only by decentering it onto other dimensions
and registers. A language is never closed upon itself, except as a function of
its impotence."[77]

Perhaps this time we can resist the temptation to say that the Internet represents a philosophical advance by the nature of its form. Instead there is a
need to recognize the many moments throughout history that people have
been misled into thinking that technology alone is a solution to an evolutionary problem or a source of intellectual insight. This technological imaginary
has functioned repeatedly as a screen onto which social desire is projected
and answered by a market economy driven by a continual need to grow. Factor in the quite human tendency to gravitate toward transformative promise
and unified consciousness, and the embrace of cyberspace becomes nearly an
inevitability. Resisting this embrace requires individual insight to be sure. But
it will also take the collective intelligence and critical acumen that a distributed conversation—a network of commentators—can provide. Far from an
isolating machine of decontextualized "pure" experience, cyberspace does
indeed offer the possibility of a type of community. Again, not the liberalized
"town hall" experience of communities on earth or the undifferentiated
"public sphere" of an artificially unified populous. Cyberspace offers people
a particular way of being together while not being together. More significantly the character and means of its experience are themselves changing. For
this reason it is important to resist closure in any discussion of such a
dynamic phenomenon.

Notes

1. Martin Heidegger, *The Question of Technology*, trans. William Lovitt (New
York: Harper and Row, 1977).
2. Leo Marx, "The Idea of Technology and Postmodern Pessimism," in *Technology, Pessimism, and Postmodernism*, ed. Yaron Ezrahi, Everett Mendelsohn, Howard
Segal, and Harold P. Segal (Amherst, Mass.: University of Massachusetts Press,
1994), 14.
3. Marx, "The Idea of Technology and Postmodern Pessimism," 15.
4. Marx, "The Idea of Technology and Postmodern Pessimism," 19.
5. Andrew Feenberg, *Critical Theory of Technology* (New York: Oxford
University Press, 1991); Andrew Feenberg and Alastair Hannay, eds., *Technology and
the Politics of Knowledge* (Bloomington and Indianapolis: Indiana University Press,
1995); Andrew Feenberg, *Questioning Technology* (New York and London: Routledge,
1998).

6. Martin Heidegger, *Being and Time*, trans. John Macquarrie and Edward Robinson (New York: Harper and Row, 1962), 41.

7. Jacques Ellul, *The Technological System*, trans. Joachim Neugroschel (New York: Continuum, 1980).

8. Andrew Ross, *Strange Weather: Culture, Science, and Technology in the Age of Limits* (London: Verso, 1991), 10.

9. Ross, *Strange Weather*, 10.

10. Sandra Harding, *Is Science Multicultural? Postcolonialisms, Feminisms, Epistemologies* (Bloomington and Indianapolis: University of Indiana, 1998).

11. Laura Mulvey, *Visual and Other Pleasures* (Bloomington: Indiana University Press, 1989); Teresa De Lauretis, *Technologies of Gender: Essays on Theory, Film, and Fiction* (Bloomington: Indiana University Press, 1987).

12. See Ezrahi et al., eds., *Technology, Pessimism, and Postmodernism*.

13. Michel Foucault, *Discipline and Punish*, trans. Alan Sheridan (New York: Pantheon, 1977).

14. Arthur Kroker, Michael A. Weinstein, *Data Trash: The Theory of the Virtual Class* (New York: St. Martin's Press, 1994), 4.

15. Nicholas Negroponte, *Being Digital* (Cambridge, Mass.: MIT Press, 1995); Mark Stefik, *Internet Dreams: Archetypes, Myths, and Metaphors* (Cambridge, Mass.: MIT Press, 1996); Peter Lunenfeld, ed., *The Digital Dialectic: New Essays on New Media* (Cambridge, Mass.: MIT Press, 1999); and Timothy Druckrey, *Electronic Culture: Technology and Visual Representation* (New York: Aperture, 1996).

16. Bill Gates, *Business@the Speed of Thought: Using a Digital Nervous System* (New York: Warner Books, 1999).

17. Gates, *Business@the Speed of Thought*, 99.

18. Michael Heim, "The Cyberspace Dialectic," in *The Digital Dialectic: New Essays on New Media*, ed. Peter Lunenfeld (Cambridge, Mass.: MIT Press, 1999), 33.

19. Paulina Borsook, *Cyberselfish: A Critical Romp Through the Terrible Libertarian Culture of High Tech* (New York: Public Affairs, 2000).

20. Borsook, *Cyberselfish*, 16.

21. Borsook, *Cyberselfish*, 130.

22. Borsook, *Cyberselfish*, 148.

23. R. L. Rutsky, *High Technē: Art and Technology from the Machine Aesthetic to the Posthuman* (Minneapolis: University of Minnesota Press, 1999), 130.

24. Mitch Kapor and John Perry Barlow, as quoted in William J. Mitchell, *City of Bits: Space, Place, and the Infobahn* (Cambridge, Mass., and London: MIT Press, 1995), 136.

25. Mitchell, *City of Bits*, 8.

26. Mitchell, *City of Bits*, 30.

27. Lunenfeld, ed., *The Digital Dialectic*, xix.

28. Lev Manovitch, "What Is Digital Cinema?" in Lunenfelt, *The Digital Dialectic*, 178.

29. Mitchell, *City of Bits*, 103.

30. Mitchell, *City of Bits*, 138.

31. James Brook and Ian Boal, eds., *Resisting the Virtual Life: The Culture and Politics of Information* (San Francisco: City Lights Books, 1995); Bill McKibben, *The Age*

of Missing Information (New York: Plume, 1993); Brian Loader, ed., *Cyberspace Divide: Equality, Agency, and Policy in the Information Society* (London and New York: Routledge, 1997); Chris Toulouse and Timothy W. Luke, eds., *The Politics of Cyberspace* (New York and London: Routledge, 1998); and Robert Markley, ed., *Virtual Realities and Their Discontents* (Baltimore: Johns Hopkins Press, 1995).

32. Ben Bagdikian, *The Media Monopoly*, 4th ed. (Boston: Beacon Press, 1992).

33. Clifford Stoll, *Silicon Snake Oil: Second Thoughts on the Information Highway* (New York: Doubleday 1995), 3.

34. Stoll, *Silicon Snake Oil*, 4.

35. Roberta Furger, *Does Jane Compute? Preserving Our Daughters' Place in the Cyber Revolution* (New York: Time-Warner Books, 1998).

36. Sherry Turkle, *Life on the Screen: Identity in the Age of the Internet* (New York: Touchstone, 1995); Anne Balsamo, *Technologies of the Gendered Body: Reading Cyborg Women* (Durham, N.C., and London: Duke University Press, 1995).

37. Donna Haraway, "A Manifesto for Cyborgs: Science, Technology, and Socialist Feminism," *Socialist Review*, 80.2 (1985): 65–108.

38. Donna Haraway, "The Persistence of Vision," in *The Visual Culture Reader*, ed. Nicholas Mirzoeff (New York and London: Routledge, 1998), 192.

39. Paul Virilio, "Speed and Information: Cyberspace Alarm!" http://www.dds.nl/~n5m/texts/virilio.htm.

40. Joseph Lockard, "Progressive Politics, Electronic Individualism, and the Myth of the Virtual Community," in *Internet Culture*, ed. David Porter (New York and London: Routledge, 1997), 227.

41. Cameron Bailey, "Virtual Skin: Articulating Race in Cyberspace," in *Immersed in Technology*, ed. Mary Anne Moser (Cambridge, Mass.: MIT Press, 1996), 38. See also Beth E. Kolko, Lisa Nakamura, and Gilbert R. Rodman, eds., *Race in Cyberspace* (London and New York: Routledge, 2000); Sarah E. Chin, *Technology and the Logic of American Racism* (New York: Continuum, 2000).

42. George P. Landow, *Hypertext 2.0: The Convergence of Contemporary Critical Theory and Technology* (Baltimore: Johns Hopkins Press, 1995).

43. Richard A. Lanham, *The Electronic Word: Democracy, Technology, and the Arts* (Chicago: University of Chicago Press, 1993).

44. Landow, *Hypertext 2.0*, 3.

45. Landow, *Hypertext 2.0*, 3.

46. Turkle, *Life on the Screen*, 17.

47. Turkle, *Life on the Screen*, 18.

48. Mark Poster, *The Mode of Information: Poststructuralism and Social Context* (Chicago: University of Chicago Press, 1990).

49. Anna Sampaio and Janni Aragon, "To Boldly Go (Where No Man Has Gone Before): Women and Politics in Cyberspace," in *The Politics of Cyberspace*, ed. Chris Toulouse and Tim Luke (New York and London: Routledge, 1998).

50. Sampaio and Aragon, "To Boldly Go (Where No Man Has Gone Before)," 154.

51. Sampaio and Aragon, "To Boldly Go (Where No Man Has Gone Before)," 150.

52. Bill Nichols, "The Work of Culture in the Age of Cybernetic Systems," in *Electronic Culture: Technology and Visual Representation*, ed. Timothy Druckrey (New

York: Aperture, 1996), 131. See also David Bell and Barbara Kennedy, eds., *The Cybercultures Reader* (London and New York: Routledge, 2000); Ken Goldberg, ed., *The Robot in the Garden: Telerobotics and Telepistemology in the Age of the Internet* (Cambridge, Mass.: MIT Press, 2000).

53. Richard Grusin, "What Is an Electronic Author? Theory and Technological Fallacy," in *Virtual Realities and Their Discontents*, ed. Markley, 42. See also Stephanie Gibson and Ollie Oviedo, eds., *The Emerging Cyberculture: Literacy, Paradigm, and Paradox* (Cresskill, N.J.: Hampton Press, 2000).

54. Grusin, "What Is an Electronic Author?" 52.

55. Landow, *Hypertext 2.0,* 107.

56. Jeremy Rifkin, *The Age of Access: The New Culture of Hypercapitalism, Where All of Life Is a Paid-For Experience* (New York: Putnam, 2000), 194.

57. Rifkin, *The Age of Access,* 194.

58. Robert Markley, "Boundaries: Mathematics, Alienation, and the Metaphysics of Cyberspace," in *Virtual Realities and Their Discontents*, ed. Markley, 56.

59. Markley, ed., *Virtual Realities and Their Discontents,* 4.

60. Fredric Jameson, "Progress versus Utopia; or, Can We Imagine the Future?" in *Art After Modernism: Rethinking Representation*, ed. Brian Wallis (New York: The New Museum, 1984).

61. William Gibson, *Neuromancer* (New York: Ace Books, 1994); Bruce Sterling, *Heavy Weather* (New York: Bantam Books, 1996).

62. Ross, *Strange Weather,* 8.

63. Dave Healy, "Cyberspace and Place: The Internet as Middle Landscape and Electronic Frontier," in *Internet Culture*, ed. Porter, 57.

64. Howard Rheingold, *The Virtual Community: Homesteading on the Electronic Frontier* (Addison-Wesley, 1993). For a critical discussion of Internet "space" and "community" see Michael Margolis and David Resnick, *Politics as Usual: The Cyberspace "Revolution,"* (Thousand Oaks, Calif.: Sage, 2000); Ann Travers, *Writing the Public in Cyberspace: Redefining Inclusion on the Net* (London and New York: Garland Publishing, 2000).

65. Rheingold, *The Virtual Community,* 24.

66. Rheingold, *The Virtual Community,* 10.

67. Porter, ed., *Internet Culture,* 14.

68. Jeffrey Fisher, "The Postmodern Paradiso: Dante, Cyberpunk, and the Technosophy of Cyberspace," in *Internet Culture*, ed. Porter, 150.

69. David Tomas, "Old Rituals for New Space: Rites and Passages in William Gibson's Cultural Model of Cyberspace," in *Cyberspace: First Steps*, ed. Michael Benedikt (Cambridge, Mass.: MIT Press, 1991), 32.

70. Marcos Novak, "Liquid Architecture in Cyberspace," in *Cyberspace*, ed. Benedikt, 225.

71. Benjamin Woolley, *Virtual Worlds: A Journey in Hype and Hyperreality* (New York: Penguin, 1992). An incisive and more detailed analysis of Heim (note 72) and Woolley appears in Markley, ed., *Virtual Realities and Their Discontents*, 55–60.

72. Michael Heim, *The Metaphysics of Virtual Reality* (London and New York: Oxford University Press), 94.

73. Markley, ed., *Virtual Realities and Their Discontents,* 4.

74. Richard Coyne, *Technoromanticism: Digital Narrative, Holism, and the Romance of the Real* (Cambridge, Mass.: MIT Press, 1999), 29.

75. Michael Heim, "The Cyberspace Dialectic," in *The Digital Dialectic*, ed. Lunenfeld, 41.

76. Gilles Deleuze and Felix Guattari, *A Thousand Plateaus: Capitalism and Schizophrenia* (Minneapolis: University of Minnesota, 1988), 9.

77. Deleuze and Guattari, *A Thousand Plateaus*, 8.

7

Broken Promises and
Democratic Possibilities

The future was and remains the quintessential American art form. Other
nations sit back and let their futures happen; we construct ours.

David Gelernter, professor of computer science, Yale University

I expect science to be conquered by market forces just like the Internet
was, so that science becomes indistinguishable from product development. There will still be a few guys in ivory towers pursuing basic questions, but they'll be regarded as artsy cranks who have outlived their
time.

Bruce Sterling, author, *Distraction*

Soon you will be able to face anyone on earth and speak, while your
translation box (something like a Palm) will announce what you've
said—in their language. This will be good for us. There is a tendency to
feel that people who cannot talk to you are not quite human.

Kim Stanley Robinson, author,
The Red Mars/Green Mars/Blue Mars trilogy

By 2100, Moore's law will have given us tiny quantum computers powerful enough to upload a human soul.

Frank Tipler, author, *The Physics of Mortality*

WE LIVE IN AN ERA in which technology is seen as a force of revolutionary change and endless possibility. Digital media have fostered new
forms of communication, commerce, and entertainment that have changed
the way people think, work, and play. At the same time, biomedical advances

have altered the way we view disease, conception, and mortality. Computers and digital networks enable new approaches to education that empower students and teachers alike, while yielding unprecedented efficiencies through mechanized instruction. Citizens from the far reaches of the nation or in countries around the world are now able to converse and exchange views on the World Wide Web in a way that promises an enrichment of free speech and democracy on a monumental scale. Indeed, the very way community is understood has been changed by the growth of virtual environments. This is the rhetoric of the digital revolution.

But before one gets too carried away with the utopian vision of this digital future, it is important to acknowledge its dark side. The reduction of communication, health care, education, community, and democracy to a vocabulary of electrical impulses has not been a neutral occurrence, for in the process of digitizing these institutions and social formations they have been transformed into commercial material. The Internet is hardly a "free" medium, even in the most generous of interpretations. One needs a computer, telephone line, and a service provider to even begin connecting. From then on one's use is metered, monitored, and tracked in databases that send one a bill on one hand, while selling information about users with the other. That is, if one has the resources, knowledge, and the technical capability to enter cyberspace. The fact remains that this purportedly transformative technology is used by a select minority of the world's population, and that Internet use within the United States is low among the poor, the uneducated, certain communities of color, and in rural regions. Seen in this light, "cyberdemocracy" is either a cruel joke or a "consensual hallucination."

The failure of digital democracy results not so much from any inherent quality of the computer medium, as it does from the social conditions into which the computer was introduced. Of central importance is the role of commerce in promoting cyberspace as a consumerist fantasyland and a marketing utopia. In addition to the ubiquitous promotion of actual hardware, software, and network services, the discourse of digital media does something far more powerful. It both creates and satisfies the desire for a better life, a wealthier existence, and a more peaceful world. In other words, cyberspace and new technology promise a utopia. But this is not the kind of philosophical utopia one normally considers. Instead this is a vision of a better world made available for a price. Of significance in all of this is the extent to which cyberspace is both a product and a medium for products.

As product and medium, the Internet is perfectly suited for adaptation within an institution like education. With a market representing nearly $700 billion per year, it's no surprise that savvy technology business people joined the chorus of reformers calling for greater efficiencies and more "entrepreneurial" teaching practices in schools. The result is a national public educational system in which advertising and product placement are now integral to the curriculum and other activities in many schools. Colleges and universities, bracing for the echo boom demographic crunch, willingly accept corporate solutions for maximizing teacher efficiency with mechanized instruction and distance learning. Meanwhile, corporations are recognizing the strategic importance of university research sponsorship in an era in which "knowledge industries" demand a steady source of new ideas and products.

Rather than democratizing education, technology is widening the gap between wealthy and poor institutions—as those with the least resources are least likely to afford technology. Schools that comprised more than 90 percent of students of color had a student-to-computer ratio of 17-to-1 in 2000, compared with the national average of 10-to-1. The historic lag in the introduction of computers into many rural and urban schools is yet another symptom of the savage inequalities in school funding from district to district. These inequities established the framework for differentials in computer access and usage that favored middle-class and wealthy students, contributing to what is now termed the "World White Web." But the introduction of computer technology into the classroom did much more. It provided technology companies a reason to enter education commercially and a way for business to get involved in school policy. During the 1990s, not only did schools come to operate like corporations, but the content of what was taught began to change to accommodate industry needs. From elementary and secondary schools to colleges and universities, the last decade of the twentieth century signaled a dramatic reorientation of education in a more meritocratic and vocational direction. With these changes came more authoritarian attitudes toward young people and increasingly sophisticated means of regulating student behavior. As established corporate power structures solidified their lock on education, voices of dissent or difference became ever more silent.

Meanwhile, outside the classroom and around the world a growing digital divide emerged between information haves and have-nots, with vast populations unable to join the technological revolution. As the Internet became a dominant medium of government, business, and personal communication, it eroded democracy by excluding certain populations and nations from the dialogue so central to an egalitarian society. One hundred companies, mostly based in the United States, conduct 90 percent of e-commerce. In the face of these enormous inequities, the dominant rhetoric of the Internet business community during the late 1990s was one of optimism and celebration. As the cover of the January 2000 *Wired* magazine read, "The Future Gets Fun Again." Certainly for technology entrepreneurs and investors making millions on inflated stock prices, looking ahead seemed tantalizing.

With the recent deflations in the dot-com sector, this boosterism has been tempered somewhat. Nevertheless, the new digital class promotes its view of cybersociety and high technology in a way that blends the sensibilities of technological determinism with an arrogant libertarianism into the new "hybrid orthodoxy" of the information age. This Silicon Valley ideology is characterized by a valorization of technological entrepreneurship, a contempt for government, and a disdain of philanthropy. Paulina Borsook details the ironic tendency of the entrepreneurial digerati to deride, not only the regulatory processes of government, but all public institutions, especially schools and universities.[1] Like much anti-government thinking, the techno-libertarian crowd gives itself credit for its performance in the marketplace, attributing this success to intelligence, drive, and hard work. As Borsook points out, "without government, there would be no internet," adding,

> Further there would be no microprocessor industry, the fount of Silicon Valley's prosperity (early computers sprang out of government funded electronics research). There would also be no major research universities cranking out qualified tech workers: Stanford, Berkeley, MIT, and Carnegie–Melon get access to state-of-the-art equipment plus R&D, courtesy of tax-reduced academic–industry consortia and taxpayer funded grants and fellowships.[2]

In his infamous "Declaration of Independence in Cyberspace" cyberlibertarian patriarch John Perry Barlow asserted that regulatory authorities had "declared war on Cyberspace," in response to which he exhorted, "Governments of the Industrial World, you weary giants of flesh and steel, I come from Cyberspace, the new home of the mind. On behalf of the future, I ask you of the past to leave us alone."[3]

Such remarks might seem humorous if they didn't carry such sobering implications. Complementing the digerati's celebration of its own achievement has been a marked disdain for those who fail to achieve—a meritocratic belief that those at the bottom of society deserve to be there. This is manifest in the profound reluctance of Silicon Valley corporations and their executives to engage in philanthropic endeavors. In the 1990s, personal wealth in the Silicon Valley grew by $100 billion, creating 65,000 millionaires and a dozen billionaires. During that period, personal giving stood at 2 percent of annual income as corporate giving dropped from 1.1 percent in 1993 to 0.9 in 1997.[4] Significant declines in wealth resulted from the dot-com meltdowns in 2000 and 2001. Yet a residual arrogance persists. Part of this can be attributed to the relative youth of Silicon Valley wealthy and their inexperience with giving. But the stinginess also results from workaholism, alienation from community, and a scorn for any of the messy realities that lie outside the digital domain. Consequently, while espousing a rhetoric of equality and democracy, this new mandarin class of young, primarily White, male technophiles constructs itself at a distance from those who lack the money, education, or access to new technology. Commenting on this solipsism of the new digerati, Joe Lockard cautions that, despite the advances of technology, "we shall continue to live in a material world where 'freedom-to-be' is an assertion of superior privilege over those who, for reasons of poverty and education, will never have the ability to advance assertions of such freedom."[5]

Living in the Material World

Much of this book has been devoted to an analysis of digital culture, and its relentless co-optation by corporations. It would be a mistake to assume that the possibilities for a digital democracy are lost, however. They are quite real, but they do not emanate from technology alone. Cyberspace simply has provided a staging ground for antidemocratic maneuvers that exacerbate social inequalities. Admittedly, its formal novelty has enabled these maneuvers to occur in unprecedented ways. Yet the forces that drive these inequitable tendencies lie outside the virtual world. They are embedded in the material institutions and social formations of the nonvirtual world, as well as the subjectivities of the people who live in that exterior world. Understanding the profound manner in which cyberspace is a social construction lies at the center of its democratization.

The restoration of an egalitarian public sphere will be possible in virtual technologies, digital education, and cyberdemocracy—only if a clear and necessary link is recognized between the online world and the material world to which it is tethered. Moreover, these inherently political answers will not emerge from the usual sources. As the centrist government in Washington is handed back and forth between Republican and Democratic hands, there is little indication that meaningful social change will emanate from political parties. For this reason it is more important than ever to seize the initiative rather than wait for others to act.

This new initiative must combine an appeal to an ethics rarely evoked in the discourse of cyberspace. Rather than appealing to a "universal" language of mathematics, which would reduce the myriad human differences of age, ethnicity, income, gender, sexual practice, and country of origin to a vocabulary of zeros and ones, equality on the Net needs to be articulated through the connections it makes to the agents that call its telepresence into existence. Given such a model, it is incumbent upon digital activists—as opposed to pseudo-political netizens—to reassert their roles in defining how cyberspace is understood and used. After all, it was *Wired* magazine's formulation of the netizen that helped drive the myth of the virtual community and online public spaces as sites of civic ritual and democratic participation. Rarely discussed was the fact that the most prodigious organizing forces in today's society both online and off are commercial market cohorts, not warm and fuzzy communities. As rival Internet providers evoke geographical metaphors like "home page" and "electronic village" to create the appearance of democratic polis, providers like America Online and Earthlink are simultaneously developing ways to frustrate the ability of subscribers to exit their service, or they are selling the addresses of their "communities" to advertisers as upscale demographic targets. In both instances, community becomes commodified as something attained for a price.

Michael Heim writes, "We are more equal on the net because we can either ignore or create the body that appears in cyberspace."[6] But what Heim and numerous others fail to acknowledge is the way that the authors of the cyberbody remain in the material world—their identities, values, and prejudices largely undisturbed by brief encounters in the virtual world. To many critics of the virtual society, this constitutes more than a benign lapse into cyberfantasyland. As Ann Travers writes,

> What assumptions are we perpetuating by this celebration of lack of embodiment in cyberspace? Denial of the body has been a foundation of forms of social and political engineering that have cruelly ignored the concerns of those for whom this denial is not possible—women, children, the elderly, the poor. Exalting the denial of the body reinforces the current gendered, raced, and classed division of labor.[7]

But it wouldn't be in the interest of Microsoft or Intel to dwell on such exigencies. Instead the public is overwhelmed by an avalanche of advertisements evoking the liberating potentials of Internet communications. This is what makes the hype so troubling. Beyond claims that the Net constitutes a novelty, convenience, or diversion has been the appropriation of formerly sacred values of community, democracy, and freedom. Perhaps in an age in which the genuine enjoyment of these virtues has been so undermined, people are more likely to accept them in simulated form. Arthur Kroker captures these sentiments in suggesting that cyberspace has been overtaken by "the predatory business interests of a virtual class, which might pay lip service to the growth of online communities on a global basis, but which is devoted in actuality to shutting down the anarchy of the Net in favor of virtualized (commercial) exchange."[8]

Reclaiming Democracy

Given this history, it is essential for progressive activists to reclaim the notion of democracy in cyberspace. Not the idealized democracy of unproblematic online verisimilitude, but a democracy defined by continual struggle, change, and critical revision. This is not to suggest a return to nostalgic origins, but to propose a democratic imaginary yet unrealized in human history. It certainly does not mean subscribing to the romanticized and universalizing views of democracy and community so common in cyberdiscourse. The task has both political and ethical dimensions. In political terms the common shortcoming of all hegemonic regimes (including utopian ones) is their implication of totalizing ideology or subjectivity. This problem becomes particularly evident in the struggle described throughout this book between those who uncritically espouse the Microsoft version of "virtual community" and those who see that brand of cyberdemocracy as a commercialized and exclusionary façade. In contrast, a true digital democracy would define itself on all levels in pluralistic terms—as a negotiation between the universalizing tendencies of Net communities and the very real ways that differences operate within them. This negotiated approach resembles the rhizomatic spirit of the Internet, to be sure, but its spirit is not defined by any technology.

This is where the ethical dimension of cyberdemocracy comes in. Beyond establishing a utopian program based solely on what might be, and beyond an aesthetic attachment to transcendental ideals, lies a commitment among the members of a democracy to their mutual project. This is hardly a new idea, but it raises questions that resist easy resolution. Many feminists correctly have argued that it is impossible ever to separate the public (online) from the private (offline).[9] Even more problematic is the difficulty of determining exactly "what works" in the pragmatic scheme. Indeed the entire adaptive program of pragmatic ethics is thrown into question by the poststructuralist questioning of "according to whom?" and "in whose interests?"[10]

Needed is a way to integrate public and individual realms without succumbing to a universalizing reason. The first step in this process lies in recognizing the importance of identity-based social movements and constituency groupings in both online and offline worlds.

It bears reiteration that in seeking to establish linkages among online groups, care must be taken to avoid merging one identity into another. This requires a form of ethics premised on a moral "respect" for the Other in the face of totalizing impulses. Suspicious of how the concept of ethics can be deployed as a means of ideological control, Emmanuel Levinas discusses the cautions necessary in forging the relationship of ethics and egalitarian politics.[11] According to Levinas the key is a form of respectful *dialogue* that allows the Other to retain an external alterity. Again, this can be a tricky process because parties rarely enter dialogues on even footing. Without denying that such asymmetries exist, Levinas suggests a moral attitude toward the civic subjectivity. It is not an attribute of an autonomous ego, but a substance fashioned in a relationship of mutual dependence.[12] More specifically, "ethics redefines subjectivity as heteronomous responsibility in contrast to autonomous freedom."[13]

Achieving this level of cyberdemocracy will mean activating mechanisms of collective agency that encourage people to act politically online. This is what tells people that their actions have an impact in the face of governments and corporate bureaucracies. It is a deeply pedagogical task in that it requires an active disavowal of old habits and diminished expectations. To approach this task one must first examine in more detail the structures that hold in place such apathy and indifference to political involvement. The most damaging impediments to a genuine cyberdemocracy can be summarized in three categories: *objectification, rationalization,* and *commodification.*[14]

Objectification can be described as the process through which people come to be seen as passive and manipulable objects, rather than active and autonomous subjects. Objectification perpetuates a fatalism that tells people they can do little to alter the course of history or their own lives. This ideology of passive spectatorship is deployed in many forms including the mass media. Movies, television, magazines, and newspapers suggest that the production of ideas and images is something that is always done by someone else. Although great claims are made about the participatory and interactive potentials of the Internet, the vast majority of Internet use is mediated by large corporations that provide the illusion of choice via selection from a range of predetermined options. Shopping online should not be confused with personal freedom.

Rationalization is the process often associated with modernism, structuralism, and functionalism that imposes bureaucratic regulation, surveillance, and measurement on human activity for the purpose of increasing efficiency. In this scheme, people submit to larger structures in the presumed interest of social progress. Ask any newcomer to the Internet about the rules, protocols, and vocabularies that structure access and navigation—only to become naturalized and forgotten with subsequent use. What often gets lost in the process is any sense of accountability or any ability of the individual or group to challenge the common order. Beyond being told that they cannot make a difference, this thinking implicitly tells citizens that they should not rock the boat, cause trouble, upset the system.

Commodification foregrounds valuation and exchange as elements of objectification and rationalization. It encourages acquisition and consumption as means of personal satisfaction, while on a structural level promoting hierarchies of production and distribution. On a broader scale commodification frustrates community ethos by encouraging competitive acquisition. Debilitating fictions of "making it" and "the good life" are defined in terms of solitary consumption rather than civic concern. Indeed, consumption and greed are the significant forces with which to contend in cyberculture.

As asserted repeatedly in these pages, one of the most celebrated attributes of cyberspace has been the appeal to civic solidarity at a time when social relations in the "real" world seem to be falling apart. This is what motivates much of the discourse of the "virtual community." Unfortunately the totalizing aspects of the utopian global village undermine any assertions of diversity or equality. Needed is an approach to cyberdemocracy that is guided by ethics—but not just any ethics. Like so much cyberwriting, much of the contemporary discourse of ethics supports itself by holding up the promise of foundational truths or rational structures of analysis.

Needed is an approach to ethics that acknowledges both the constructed character of meaning and the viability of cultural difference as a positive element in social organization. A single viewpoint can never satisfy the needs of all people. Such monolithic thinking is what blinds colonial powers to the tyrannies they project.

"Radical democracy" can provide that ethical project. Indeed, democracy is a process that depends on participation—the willingness and belief that the actions, voices, and votes of individuals can have an effect on the collective totality. In part this constitutes an exercise in political imagination; in part it is a consequence of positive agency that convinces an active citizenry that its constituents are their own rulers. To a large extent, what makes this process of democracy work is a faith in its fairness, in a belief that participation is unstymied by inequity and injustice. This is what gives the practice of democracy its moral character. Not a belief in a common culture that supplants all other, not a faith in an unproblematic form of patriotism that blindly follows symbols, not a reverence for a dehistoricized heritage. Radical democracy achieves its ethical dimension in its invitation for participation from all quarters, and by necessity its resistance to racism, homophobia, commodification, sexism, and all other forms of objectifying, colonizing, and dehumanizing behavior. Within this environment citizens are bound by the responsibility to act on their beliefs, rather than waiting for others to do so for them.[15] Here democracy is both the means by which the oppressed come to know their oppression, and the vehicle through which they struggle to find methods for change.

Notes

1. Paulina Borsook, *Cyberselfish: A Critical Romp Through the Terrible Libertarian Culture of High Tech* (New York: Public Affairs, 2000). See also Michael Margolis and David Resnick, *Politics as Usual: The Cyberspace "Revolution"* (Thousand Oaks, Calif.: Sage, 2000); Ann Travers, *Writing the Public in Cyberspace: Redefining Inclusion on the Net* (London and New York: Garland Publishing, 2000).

2. Borsook, *Cyberselfish*, 6.

3. Borsook, *Cyberselfish*, 153.

4. Borsook, *Cyberselfish*, 174.

5. Joe Lockard, "Babel Machines and Electronic Universalisms," in *Race in Cyberspace*, ed. Beth Kolko, Lisa Nakamura, and Gilbert Rodman (New York and London: Routledge, 2000), 180. See also Stephanie Gibson and Ollie Oviedo, eds., *The Emerging Cyberculture: Literacy, Paradigm, and Paradox* (Cresskill, N.J.: Hampton Press, 2000); Ken Goldberg, ed., *The Robot in the Garden: Telerobotics and Telepistemology in the Age of the Internet* (Cambridge, Mass.: MIT Press, 2000).

6. Michael Heim, as quoted in Ann Travers, *Writing the Public in Cyberspace: Redefining Inclusion on the Net* (New York and London: Garland, 2000), 2.

7. Travers, *Writing the Public in Cyberspace*, 7.

8. Arthur Kroker, as quoted in Andrew Calcutt, *White Noise: An A–Z of the Contradictions in Cyberculture* (New York: St. Martin's Press, 1999), 36.

9. A critique of Rorty following this argument is found in Nancy Fraser, *Unruly Practices: Power, Discourse, and Gender in Contemporary Social Theory* (Minneapolis: University of Minnesota Press, 1989), 93–112. Fraser develops a considered critique of Rorty, which problematizes his effort to sustain pragmatic and romantic autonomy.

10. This issue is discussed at length in a chapter titled "Management as Moral Technology: A Luddite Analysis," in *Foucault and Education: Discipline and Punish*, ed. Stephen J. Ball (New York: Routledge, 1990), 153–166.

11. Emmanuel Levinas, *Totality and Infinity: An Essay on Exteriority*, trans. Alphonso Lingis (Pittsburgh: Duquesne University Press, 1969), 21.

12. Robert Young, *White Mythologies: Writing History and the West* (London and New York: Routledge, 1990), 16.

13. Emmanuel Levinas, as quoted in Young, *White Mythologies*, 16.

14. Cornell West, "The New Cultural Politics of Difference," in *Out There: Marginalization and Contemporary Culture*, ed. Martha Gever, Russell Ferguson, Trinh T. Minh-ha, and Cornell West (Cambridge, Mass.: MIT Press, 1990), 35. West develops the ethical typology of objectification, rationalization, and commodification, adapted here to address cyberculture. See also David Purpel, *The Moral and Spiritual Crisis in Education* (New York: Bergin and Garvey, 1989); David Bell and Barbara Kennedy, eds., *The Cybercultures Reader* (London and New York: Routledge, 2000); Gill Kirkup et al., eds., *The Gendered Cyborg: A Reader* (London and New York: Routledge, 2000); Beth Kolko, Lisa Nakamura, and Gilbert Rodman, eds., *Race in Cyberspace* (London and New York: Routledge), 2000.

15. Chantal Mouffe, "Democratic Politics Today," *Dimensions of Radical Democ-*

racy: Pluralism, Citizenship, Community, ed. Chantal Mouffe (London: Verso, 1992), 4. See also Michael Margolis and David Resnick, *Politics as Usual: The Cyberspace "Revolution"* (Thousand Oaks, Calif.: Sage, 2000); Ann Travers, *Writing the Public in Cyberspace: Redefining Inclusion on the Net* (London and New York: Garland Publishing, 2000).

Index

African Americans, 28, 33, 39, 53
Amazon.com, 89–90
America Online, 26–27, 46
A Nation at Risk, 1, 49
Aronowitz, Stanley, 29–30, 35, 38
Asian Americans, 32–33, 38–39

Bagdikian, Benjamin, 25–26, 125
Bailey, Cameron, 36, 128
Barlow, John Perry, 10, 122–23, 135, 146
Barthes, Roland, 129, 132
Baudrillard, Jean, 88, 130
Benton Foundation, 28–29, 73
Bérubé, Michael, 7–8, 60
Bobbio, Noberto, 100–101
Bolt, David, 32, 70–71
Borsook, Paulina, 122, 146
Bush, George H. W., 46, 47, 50, 68

capitalism, 5, 13, 22, 118
Cartesian, 35, 50, 128
Castells, Manuel, 87, 106
Chomsky, Noam, 27, 104
Cisco Systems, 7, 60, 74
Clinton, William, 2, 6, 45–46, 50, 71–72
Cold War, 46, 85
colonialism, 104, 128, 135
communities, 8–9, 12, 37, 89, 133, 138
conservatives, 30, 70
corporations, 3, 45, 59
Crawford, Ray, 32, 70–71
critical pedagogy, 69–70

culture wars, 8, 45
cyberculture, 9, 17
cyberdemocracy, 91–95

deconstruction, 71, 50, 128
Deleuze, Gilles, 109, 137–38
democracy, 12, 14, 17, 26, 33, 46, 79, 147; liberal, 98–99, 100; radical, 102–3, 109, 151; socialist, 99–100
Derrida, Jacques, 129, 132
difference, 37, 71, 85
digerati, 9–10, 121–22
digital divide, 10, 23–29, 32–33, 70–72
digital literacy, 69–70, 71
diploma mills, 4, 75–76
distance learning, 66, 75, 78, 80

e-commerce, 14, 87, 125
educational reform, 2, 46–47, 49, 70
electronic frontier, 108, 123, 134
English language, 24, 27, 56
Enlightenment, 91–92, 115, 119, 124

Feenberg, Andrew, 117, 119
feminism, 57, 93, 118–19, 126–27
Fernandez, Maria, 108–9
Foucault, Michel, 9, 79, 118–19, 132
free speech, 52, 91

Gates, William, 19, 21, 37, 68, 120–21
gender, 37, 67, 107
Gibson, William, 88, 134

Gingrich, Newt, 12, 88
global village, 12, 20, 85
Gore, Albert, 12, 68, 86, 120
Guattari, Felix, 109, 137–38

hackers, 34, 107
Haraway, Donna, 35, 126–27
Harding, Sandra, 36, 118
Heim, Michael, 27, 122, 136, 148
homophobia, 128, 151
hypertext, 71, 129, 132, 136

IBM, 7, 74
imagined communities, 86–87
information economy, 60, 80
intellectual capital, 6, 17, 58–60, 76

Kimball, Roger, 50–51
knowledge industries, 30, 76, 145
Kroker, Arthur, 19, 137, 148

labor, 31, 66
Laclau, Ernesto, 102–3, 109
Landow, George, 94–95
language, 38, 138, 147
Lanham, Richard, 81–82, 94, 129–30,
    133
Latinos, 20, 33
Levinas, Immanuel, 149–50
liberals, 30, 49, 56, 58, 68
lifelong learning, 9, 71, 75
Lockard, Joseph, 37, 87, 108, 127, 147

Markel Foundation, 28, 73
Markley, Robert, 125, 133
McChesney, Robert, 25–26
McLuhan, Marshall, 12, 20, 67, 85, 121,
    130
meritocracy, 32, 46
Microsoft Corporation, 21–22, 27, 121,
    128, 137, 148
middle-class people, 37, 107
Mitchell, William, 79, 123–25
modernism, 91, 116, 121, 126, 129
Mouffe, Chantal, 102–3, 109
multiculturalism, 48, 50, 66

multinational corporations, 8, 13, 22, 17,
    59, 108, 125

Nakamura, Lisa, 37, 38
National Science Foundation, 73, 82
netiquette, 36, 128
netizen, 9–10, 121
"New World Order," 20, 27
Noble, David, 4, 7, 75–76

political correctness, 48, 50, 66
Poster, Mark, 94, 109, 130
Postman, Neil, 81, 130
postmodernism, 94, 127–28
power, 8–9, 17, 47, 79
privatization, 55, 58, 82
public sphere, 27, 91–93, 138

race, 27, 37–39, 67, 127
racism, 128, 151
Reagan, Ronald, 46–47, 49, 68, 93, 122
Republican Party, 93, 147
research, 4, 59–61, 78
Rheingold, Howard, 12, 19, 27, 88, 124,
    135
rhizome, 137, 149
Rifkin, Jeremy, 11, 23, 31, 80–81, 90, 133
Robbins, Kevin, 8–9, 55
Ross, Andrew, 57, 118, 134

Sardar, Ziauddun, 13, 104–5
Silicon Valley, 9–10, 32, 122–23, 125,
    146
social class, 37, 38, 67, 107
social inequality, 58, 87
Sterling, Bruce, 34, 134, 143
Sterne, Jonathan, 72–73
subjectivity, 17, 94, 109, 131
suburbia, 36, 72, 108
surveillance, 9, 12, 86, 127

technological instrumentalism, 115–17,
    121, 136
technologies of gender, 118, 127
tidal wave, 45, 65
Turkle, Sherry, 37, 126, 130

University of California, 60, 73, 82
University of Phoenix, 4, 7, 56, 77
U.S. Commerce Department, 5, 10, 22–23, 28–29, 31
utopia, 12, 14, 32–33, 79, 86, 136, 144

Virilio, Paul, 19, 127
virtual community, 12–13, 19, 86–87, 89, 134–35, 149, 151
virtual reality, 133, 137
visual literacy, 67–68

vocational education, 5–6, 58, 67

Webster, Frank, 8–9, 55
West, Cornel, 53–54
Western Governors University, 7, 74
White male, 30, 34, 36, 147
Whiteness, 72, 108
Whittle, Christopher, 3, 47
Wired magazine, 21, 106, 121–23, 145, 148
Woolley, Benjamin, 10, 135–36

About the Author

David Trend is professor of studio art at University of California, Irvine, and director of the University of California Institute for Research in the Arts, the funding program for arts projects and research on the nine UC campuses. Before arriving at UC Irvine in 1997, Trend was dean of creative arts at De Anza College in Cupertino, California, where he developed multimedia partnerships with schools and corporations in Silicon Valley. During the past fifteen years, Trend has been a frequent consultant for foundations, state arts and humanities councils, and the National Endowment for the Arts.

The author of over one hundred articles and essays in such periodicals as *Art in America, Cultural Studies,* and *Social Identities,* Trend is a former editor of the journals *Afterimage* and *Socialist Review* and a current editorial board member of the *Journal of Education, Pedagogy, and Cultural Studies.* Trend's books include *Cultural Pedagogy: Art/Education/Politics* (Bergin and Garvey 1992), *The Crisis of Meaning in Culture and Education* (University of Minnesota Press 1995), *Radical Democracy: Identity, Citizenship, and the State* (Routledge 1996), *Cultural Democracy: Politics, Media, New Technology* (State University of New York Press 1997), and *Reading Digital Culture* (Blackwell 2001).